IMPRESSIONIST QUILTS

GAI PERRY

C&T PUBLISHING

© Copyright 1995 Gai Perry

Developmental editing by Barbara Konzak Kuhn

Technical editing by Joyce Engels Lytle

Cover design by Morris Design, Monterey, CA

Book design by Kajun Graphics, San Francisco, CA

Illustrations by Kandy Petersen, Moraga, CA

All photography by Sharon Reisdorph, San Francisco, CA, unless otherwise noted.

Photographs on pages 8, 41, and 94, styled by Adrian Gallardo & Renee Isabelle Walker, Stephen Reed Flowers, Lafayette, CA

This book is dedicated to my family and to all my wonderfully talented Impressionist Landscape students.

Library of Congress Cataloging-in-Publication Data

Perry, Gai

Impressionist quilts: a color and design manual / by Gai Perry.

p. cm.

Includes bibliographical references.

ISBN 1-57120-003-7 (pbk.)

1. Patchwork—Patterns.   2. Quilting—Patterns.   3. Quilts—Design.
4. Landscape in art.   I. Title

TT835.P44912   1995

746.46'0433—dc20   95-16915

CIP

BURPEE is a registered trademark of W. Atlee Burpee & Company.

CHACO-LINER is a registered trademark of General Pencil Company.

MOUNTAIN MIST is a registered trademark of Stearns Technical Textiles Company.

LOW-LOFT is a registered trademark of Fairfield Processing Corporation.

Published by C&T Publishing, Inc.

P.O. Box 1456

Lafayette, California 94549

Printed in Hong Kong

10 9 8 7 6 5 4

TABLE OF CONTENTS

RAINBOWS, 1984, 36″ X 44″, GAI PERRY

This is one of my favorite quilts from my traditional period—I love the pure interaction of the solid colors.

$\mathcal{F}$OREWORD

MAKING A QUILT IS AN ACT OF LOVE. One's involvement in choosing a pattern and selecting the fabrics is both passionate and intense. The heady pleasure is multiplied and shared when a finished quilt is given to someone we care about. Although I've been an artist, antique dealer, and advertising copywriter, none of these professions have been as emotionally and artistically satisfying as being a quilter.

I took my first quilting class in 1981, about the time my youngest son was heading off to college. Quilting was going to be a nice little hobby—something to help ward off the "empty nest" syndrome. (I never dreamed, while struggling with my first quilt, that I'd go on to make over a hundred more, and become totally immersed in this enchanting craft.) For the first few years, I contentedly made Amish-style quilts and mellow-colored scrap quilts that had the look of an earlier century. But the time came when I had made a quilt using every traditional block and pattern that had interested me, so I started designing some of my own. This was fun for awhile but these new pieces were still variations on a traditional theme, and I was becoming restless. By the fall of 1990, I had lost interest in quiltmaking and thought about going back to painting. I hesitated for one reason: I knew, in my heart, I was a much better quilter than a painter. That's when I decided to explore contemporary quilt design.

While struggling with the problems of "what" and "how," I came across a book entitled *The Fine Art of Quilting* by Vicki Barker and Tessa Bird. Included in the book was a wall hanging made by Linda Koolhass in 1984. It was an abstract design that gave the illusion of washes of color. The quilt reminded me of a window so drenched with rain that only the blurred colors of the outdoors were visible through the reflections of the raindrops. Impressionism! That was it! I wondered if it was possible to design a quilt that looked like an Impressionist's painting where natural elements like hills, flowers, and the sky would be recognizable. Claude Monet, the father of Impressionism, has always been one of my heroes. What a wonderful tribute this would be if I could somehow make it work.

I noticed Linda Koolhass made her quilt by repeating a diamond shape. For a quilter, this means inset piecing. For me, it's not fun to do so I translated the diamond shape into a square and set it on point. Landscapes made with straight rows of squares have always looked computer generated to me. By putting the squares point-to-point I hoped there would be better interaction of color between the squares, and a subtler blending of seam lines. Using this technique, I made ENGLISH COTTAGE GARDEN (page 14), my first Impressionist Landscape quilt. That was November of 1990. Since then, I've made dozens more and still haven't scratched the surface of design possibilities. The process is never boring. Each new quilt idea becomes a fresh canvas to explore and conquer.

When I started working on this quilt series, I never thought that I'd be able to teach the technique, much less write a how-to book. But now, after five years, I feel that I know enough about the art of creating Impressionist Landscape quilts to share it with you. The beauty of the technique is that you don't have to be a talented artist, or an expert colorist —you don't even have to be an experienced quilter. The secret lies in buying the right fabrics and because I'm a consummate consumer (and buy a lot of fabric) I can tell you how to do this.

*I*NTRODUCTION

FEW OF US WILL EVER BE FORTUNATE enough to own a great Impressionist painting or even see one in person, but there is no reason why we can't learn to make our own Impressionist work of art using fabric. This book will teach you how to blend hundreds of squares into a luminous fabric painting. There is no appliqué, no strip sewing—just simple piecing of squares on point. You will learn how to use printed fabrics to create a beautiful Impressionist masterpiece: a treasure to keep or to share.

"Hands on" means to learn by doing and it's an apt description of this book. You can read every chapter and enjoy the quilt photographs, but until you start working on one of the projects, you won't begin to comprehend the joy that can be derived from cutting little squares of printed fabric and arranging them into a garden, a meadow, or even a cascading waterfall. Working with flowers must have a universal appeal; we feel like we're communing with nature and we become so involved with the creative process that we are able, for a little while, to forget about daily routines and schedules. At the end of a two-day session, my workshop students will tell me that it is the most relaxing class they have ever taken. I find this hard to believe because I've watched them work at their design board for hours on end, cutting and rearranging the squares, and then dash into the shop to buy more fabric, or trade squares with a neighbor.

This book is arranged in sequential order with a gradual layering of information that will ultimately lead you to the completion of a successful landscape. The presentation of design, color, and fabric requirements is general in nature until you reach the individual projects. Then, detailed instructions are given for each of the wall hangings. There are very few rules; almost nothing is "written in stone" (aside from a few fabric recommendations), and you will find many opportunities to imprint your own style within the boundaries of this Impressionist Landscape technique. If you read through the book before making any fabric purchases, you'll save yourself some money. You may be a magnificent artist, a brilliant colorist, but the truth is that the best landscape quilts are made by people who willingly accept the fabric information and scour the local shops looking for that one perfect rose, tulip, or chrysanthemum.

You are about to start a beautiful quiltmaking experience. Get ready for the time of your life!

POPPY FIELD IN A HOLLOW NEAR GIVERNY, 1885
CLAUDE MONET
Juliana Cheney Edwards Collection
Courtesy, Museum of Fine Arts, Boston

WHAT IS IMPRESSIONISM?

IMPRESSIONISM IS A STYLE OF PAINTING that originated in France during the middle of the nineteenth century. Artists like Monet, Renoir, and Pizarro shocked the art world with their revolutionary approach to painting. They shunned the rigidly controlled atmosphere of the indoor studio, preferring to paint in the open air or *plen aire*. Here they captured the fragile beauty of a delicate bouquet of flowers or the elegant simplicity in a quiet country scene. The Impressionists were obsessed with natural light and their interpretation of one perfect moment frozen in time. Monet is famous for his cathedral and haystack series painted at different times of day to illustrate the changing effect of light on color.

Impressionist painters used unblended pigments and applied them directly to the canvas with short, swift brush strokes. They broke the individual elements of a painting into many separate colors to obtain a luminous impression of the whole; the effect was softened outlines, with one area blending into another. By using warm-cool color contrasts and value changes, the artists created illusions of light.

Our goal, as Impressionist Landscape quilters, is to interpret nature in a similar fashion, but with fabric rather than paint.

THE IMPRESSIONIST TECHNIQUE

One of the ways that my Impressionist Landscape technique is different from the watercolor technique is that all of the squares are placed and sewn on point rather than on square (in straight rows). Placing the square on point helps to create the illusion of a real painting. The edges of the squares soften and there is a gentler blending from one color area to another. This idea occurred to me while I was studying the Amish style of quiltmaking. If you look at the different ways in which they set the Sunshine and Shadows pattern, you will find that the quilts with the squares set on point have more sizzle and vitality. The colors are also more interactive and transmit illusions of transparency.

With my technique, you are not limited to using just one size square. You have the option of using several graduated sizes to accommodate the scale of an individual flower, or group of flowers.

Another important difference in this Impressionist technique is that many of the flower squares are cut by hand to ensure that a whole flower fills, and is centered in, each square. This may sound like a lot more work, but the end result is worth the effort.

With the Impressionist Landscape technique you are striving to create an actual picture, not an abstract arrangement of light and shadow. By using flower prints for the floral areas, leaf prints for the trees, tie-dyed and marbleized fabrics for the sky, and textured prints for hills and mountains, you can make your picture as real looking as possible without actually painting on the fabric.

MONET'S GARDEN III, 1994,
55″ X 48″, GAI PERRY

DESIGN CONCEPTS

WHILE TRYING TO THINK OF A SUBJECT for my first Impressionist quilt, I remembered a painting that I had done many years ago. The scene is of an English courtyard framed by a leaded glass window. I liked the strong vertical-diagonal lines that formed the window panes, so I used them as the focus for my quilt.

I started the landscape by cutting squares from fabrics that I thought resembled distant hills. This was an arbitrary decision, but it seemed logical to start at the horizon line where the hills would eventually blend into the meadow. From there I worked gradually into the meadow and then toward the sky.

All the squares, with the exception of a few larger ones in the foreground, were cut $2\frac{1}{4}''$ square. At the time it was another arbitrary choice, but it has proven to be just the right size to encompass a single flower.

None of the solid color fabrics that I purchased were appropriate because they looked too flat. I found tone-on-tone and multi-hued prints were more desirable because they transmit an illusion of reflected light. I also learned to use both sides of a fabric (the reverse side presents a mellower image).

◀ ENGLISH COTTAGE GARDEN, 1990, 48″ X 63″, GAI PERRY

$\mathcal{L}$ANDSCAPE TERMINOLOGY

MAKING THE FIRST IMPRESSIONIST LANDSCAPE QUILT felt like walking through a maze, but it turned out much better than I expected. The second and third landscapes were terrible, but from these three quilts came the terminology that defines my technique. It is a good idea to become familiar with these terms and definitions because, later on, I use them frequently to describe fabric choices.

BASE SQUARE: All the landscapes use a base square that measures 1¾″ when sewn. However, the size can be doubled or tripled to accommodate larger flowers. Refer to the template patterns on pages 125–126.

ON POINT: The squares, no matter what size, are always sewn on point (set at a 45° angle to the sides of the quilt) and are ultimately sewn together in diagonal rows.

NATURAL ELEMENTS: Flowers, water, trees, sky, greenery, hills, mountains; anything pertaining to nature.

VALUE-CONTRASTING AREAS: It is of the utmost importance to establish three distinct value areas (light, medium, and dark) in an Impressionist Landscape quilt. Without the contrast of these areas, the finished landscape will lack definition.

COLOR-CONTRASTING AREAS: The contrast between the warm-colored flower areas and the cool-colored areas of the skies, hills, water, and greenery. It can also refer to the contrast of saturated areas to less-saturated areas. (Refer to the RULES OF CONTRAST beginning on page 27 for further definition.)

COLOR GROUP: Each of the twelve colors on the color circle has its own group of tints, tones, and shades. The color red can range from cranberry to coral; greens can range from lime to turquoise.

COLOR-RELATED PRINTS: A selection of fabrics within one of the twelve color groups.

VALUE-GRADED PRINTS: A group of fabrics in the same color group that are arranged in sequence from the lightest to the darkest.

TONE-ON-TONE PRINTS: Prints that have two or more shades of the same color.

COLOR-DOMINANT PRINTS: Prints that have a main color but are also enriched with subtle touches of other colors.

TRANSITION: To move from one value or color area to another. It is desirable to choose prints that are value- and/or color-graded so that the transitions are gradual and softly impressionistic. This is where using both the right and reverse sides of a fabric become necessary.

FOCUS: It's always nice to have a focus in your landscape. The focus grabs the viewer's attention. It may be a path, a gate, or the stark white foam of a tumbling waterfall. You will learn that the focus can be a recognizable object or a dramatic contrast of color or value.

DISTANCE AND DEPTH: To establish a foreground, a middle ground, and a background in your landscape design, make the elements in the foreground look larger and brighter. Gradually, as the eye moves toward the horizon, the elements will become smaller, lighter, and less-clearly defined.

TRIANGLE OF LIGHT: This is another method of providing a focus. To make a triangle of light, take the lightest or brightest color in your quilt and put it in three different places to form an irregular triangle. This strategy provides a subliminal focus that leads the eye around the quilt. A good example of this triangle is WATERFALL II on page 105.

COLOR AWARENESS

WORKING WITH COLOR is one of the great passions in my life. When I'm sitting on the floor of my studio, surrounded by piles of gloriously colored fabrics, I'm in heaven! Imagine the delight for a person like myself, who was once an artist, to work in a quilting style that involves arranging hundreds of colorful squares into a fabric painting. If playing with color is one of the main reasons why you enjoy quiltmaking, you are in for a treat.

I had always chosen colors intuitively, but when I started teaching color classes to quiltmakers, my conscience told me that a more academic approach was needed and I embarked on a study of color theory. The new information not only improved my traditional work, but it helped me to formulate some of the guidelines for the Impressionist Landscape series.

Color has an enormous impact on our daily lives. Legally we can't cross a city street without the go-ahead of a green light. Color tells us when fruit is ripe or when meat has spoiled. Standing in a red room can raise a person's blood pressure; the color blue has a tranquil, soothing effect. Color preferences dictate how we dress, decorate our homes, and choose the fabric for our quilts. It was surprising to learn that we're not all born with the same physical ability to see color. Just as some people have what is called a musical ear and can translate sounds into written notes, others have "color-sensitive" eyes. These people can identify and separate a broader spectrum of colors.

While I was researching color theory, I found a little book called *The Elements of Color* by Johannes Itten and it has become my color bible. He wrote the text for art students but the information is just as valid for quiltmakers. Itten explains in simple language the complexity of color relationships. He defines a twelve-color circle and presents several rules of color harmony and contrast. He also helped me to understand that color theory works because it is based on natural laws (meaning coming from nature) of color harmony and contrast. This is also why intuitive color choices are generally successful. We are creatures of nature and we respond favorably when our color choices are in sync with the environment.

The Color Primer section on the following pages is a relevant source of information for the Impressionist Landscape technique.

COLOR PRIMER

Color is the product of light radiating in the form of invisible, magnetic wavelengths (one for each of the six spectrum colors). An object, such as a red apple, appears red because its molecular structure reflects only the red wavelength while absorbing all the others. An object that reflects all the wavelengths will appear white and an object that absorbs all the wavelengths will appear black.

The Color Circle

Isaac Newton was the first scientist to develop a color circle. This circle was based on a natural phenomenon he called a spectrum. Newton discovered that a band of colors appears when light passes through a prism. The colors maintain a natural order (one color blends into another), and he realized he could arrange the colors in a circle to illustrate this natural progression.

Since Newton's early experiments, several color circles have been developed within the divergent fields of art and science. The one presented here, and illustrated in Itten's book, is generally accepted by artists and it's the one with which I'm most comfortable.

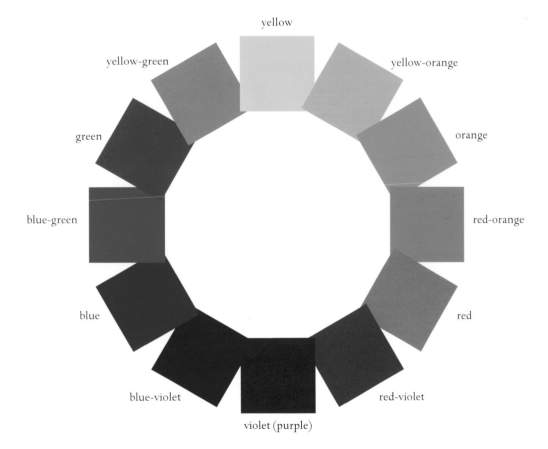

TWELVE-COLOR CIRCLE

PRIMARY COLORS: Yellow, red, and blue are the only three colors that cannot be created by mixing other colors together.

PRIMARY COLORS

SECONDARY COLORS: Violet, orange, and green are made by mixing equal parts of two primary colors. Red + blue = violet. Red + yellow = orange. Yellow + blue = green.

SECONDARY COLORS

TERTIARY COLORS: Yellow-green, red-violet, blue-green, yellow-orange, blue-violet, and red-orange are created by mixing equal parts of a primary color with a secondary color. Yellow + orange = yellow-orange.

TERTIARY COLORS

WARM AND COOL COLORS: The color circle is equally divided into warm and cool colors. The warm reds, yellows, and oranges have an aura of vitality and energy. They tend to come forward and give the illusion of occupying more space than cool colors. The cool blues, greens, and violets recede; they tend to transmit feelings of serenity and calm.

WARM COLORS

COOL COLORS

Color Terminology

HUE: Another term for the name of a color.

VALUE: The amount of black or white added to a color to make it appear darker or lighter. The value of any fabric is determined by whatever color is put next to it. Often it becomes difficult to determine the value of a fabric because its relative value keeps changing. In one quilt block it could be the darkest value while in another block it could be the medium value.

SATURATION: The purity of a color. Saturation and chroma have the same meaning and are interchangeable.

PURE COLORS: The twelve colors of the color circle are pure colors. Pure colors have not been altered by the addition of black or white to weaken their character. Quilt-makers generally avoid using large amounts of pure colors because they are too intense to be universally appealing. You can use small touches of pure color to add sparkling contrast to surrounding, less-saturated colors.

Changing Pure Colors

TINTS: Adding white creates tinted colors.

TINTS

An equal amount of white has been added to the primary and secondary colors.

SHADES: Adding black creates shaded colors.

SHADES

An equal amount of black has been added to the primary and secondary colors.

TONES: Adding blends of black and white (gray) creates toned colors.

TONES

An equal amount of gray has been added to the primary and secondary colors.

Harmonious Color Combinations

Harmony implies balance; a harmonious color scheme refers to a group of colors that have a pleasing relationship to each other. But, because color harmony is also subjective, you will often use your personal preferences when selecting colors for a quilt. The following groups of color harmonies relate directly to the color circle.

COMPLEMENTARY COLORS: Colors that are directly opposite each other on the color circle. An example is blue and orange.

COMPLEMENTARY COLORS

SPLIT-COMPLEMENTARY COLORS: Choose any color on the circle and then locate its complement. The colors on either side of the complement are the split complements. If you choose red, the split complements are yellow-green and blue-green.

SPLIT-COMPLEMENTARY COLORS

TRIAD COLORS: Any three colors that form an equilateral triangle on the color circle. An example of a triad is red-violet, blue-green, and yellow-orange.

TRIAD COLORS

TETRAD COLORS: Any four colors that form a square or rectangle on the color circle. An example of a square is green, yellow-orange, blue-violet, and red. An example of a rectangle is yellow-green, yellow-orange, red-violet, and blue-violet.

TETRAD COLORS

Color Schemes

ACHROMATIC: Without color. A quilt made in shades and tones of white, black, and gray is achromatic.

ACHROMATIC

NEUTRALS: Creamy tints and tones of tan, gray, and beige. By using mellow, pastel-tinted combinations of these colors you can develop a quilt that has understated elegance.

NEUTRALS

MONOCHROMATIC: An attractive range of tints, tones, and shades of one color. Depending on the warmth or coolness of the chosen color, monochromatic quilts can look either dramatic or tranquil.

MONOCHROMATIC

ANALOGOUS: A combination of three or more colors that are adjacent to each other on the color circle. Analogous color schemes are pleasing to the eye because the hues are closely related and they blend well together.

ANALOGOUS

POLYCHROMATIC: Containing several colors. Most scrap quilts fall into this category.

POLYCHROMATIC

THE IMPORTANCE OF CONTRAST

COLOR WITHOUT CONTRAST is one dimensional and lacks texture. Whether we try to capture the colors of nature in a painting or in a quilt, we need to understand that nature is a constantly changing palette of contrasts. Warm-cool, light-dark, large-small, or high-low—it's the variety of these opposing contrasts that unite to create a look of compelling beauty. When you are making an Impressionist Landscape quilt, it is necessary to build in some of these contrasts. To accomplish this, you must learn what contrast is and how to make it work effectively.

Individual colors are pleasant, but when a few of them are put together a chemistry begins. By itself red is intense, but when it shares the spotlight with its green complement then both colors radiate more energy. The cool green surrounds the red and makes it appear even more vibrant. The green becomes richer and more lustrous by comparison.

Some of us are perfectly happy putting several bright contrasts in our quilts while others feel more secure using fewer and gentler contrasts. Your comfort level should be the deciding factor, but it might be fun to tweak it once in awhile just to see what happens.

In his book, Johannes Itten discusses several rules of contrast; I've put my own spin on these rules and added two more which apply directly to quiltmaking.

Photo: Gai Perry

Rules of Contrast

1. CONTRAST OF COLOR: A combination of three or more colors that are at least three spaces apart on the color circle.

CONTRAST OF COLOR

2. CONTRAST OF LIGHT-DARK COLORS: A high degree of contrast is achieved by eliminating the middle values.

CONTRAST OF LIGHT-DARK COLORS

3. CONTRAST OF COMPLEMENTARY COLORS: Putting together opposite colors of the color circle enhances the best attributes of each.

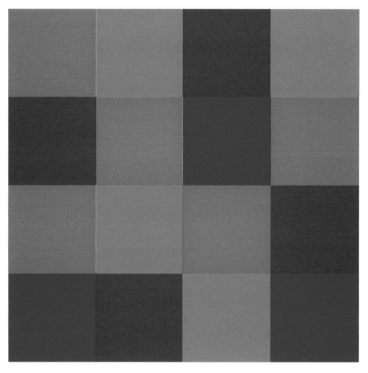

CONTRAST OF COMPLEMENTARY COLORS

4. CONTRAST OF WARM-COOL COLORS: Combining warm reds, yellows, and oranges with cool blues, and violets.

CONTRAST OF WARM-COOL COLORS

5. CONTRAST OF INTENSITY: Each color on the color circle has its own degree of intensity. You need proportionately less amounts of high-intensity colors (the warm ones) to balance the low-intensity colors (the cool ones). Yellow is the most intense color and violet is the least. The only two colors having equal intensity are red and green. They can be used in the same proportion to achieve an equal balance.

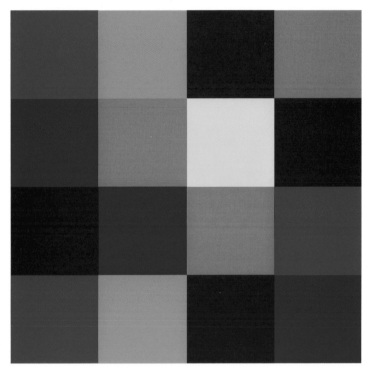

CONTRAST OF INTENSITY

6. CONTRAST OF SATURATION: The contrast between pure colors and colors that have been diluted with black or white.

CONTRAST OF SATURATION

7. CONTRAST OF FABRIC PRINT: It is important, when designing a quilt, to choose fabrics of diverse character. Most traditional quilts are enhanced by combinations of floral, geometric, and linear prints. Landscape quilts become more interesting with the addition of several different element textures.

CONTRAST OF FABRIC PRINT

8. CONTRAST OF FABRIC SCALE: Scale refers to the size of the repeated image on a fabric. Combine small, medium, and large scale prints to add movement and visual excitement to a landscape quilt.

CONTRAST OF FABRIC SCALE

COLOR THEORY APPLICATIONS

YOU MAY ASK WHY ALL THIS COLOR INFORMATION is necessary. The answer is that it gives you power! It puts you in control of your fabric choices and allows you to consciously select colors that can express a mood, an environment, or even the time of day.

For example, consider the changing colors of the sky on a summer day. Just before dawn, the sky is a soft blanket of grayish white and the landscape reflects this palette; it looks *toned* down, less saturated. To capture this time of day, look for fabrics with colors that have had black and white (gray) added to the dyes.

As the sun rises, the sky turns a rosy apricot and then gradually changes to a lovely shade of pale blue. Fabrics that have had colors *tinted* with white would be appropriate. At mid-day, when the sun is directly overhead, the sky is a brilliant azure blue. You would choose *pure* saturated colors for this time frame. By late afternoon, the sky is diffused, more turquoise in color, and at dusk, the sky explodes with sunset colors of violet, mauve, and orange. You would use colors *shaded* with black to interpret this dramatic day-into-night transition.

A vibrant landscape image is created by using mostly warm colors as in BURPEE®: HYBRID MIX on page 104. A feeling of pristine tranquillity is generated with a cool monochromatic color scheme as in FIRST WATERFALL on page 98.

The contrast of complementary colors was a favorite contrast of the Impressionists. They also consistently used the contrast of warm-cool colors, and the contrast of saturation to control the atmosphere of a scene. It would be to your advantage to find a book of Impressionist paintings. You can learn so much by just studying the pictures. A tree, a flower, or even a ripe piece of fruit was never painted with just one color. An Impressionist would use several color-related hues to define the smallest patch of grass, and flesh tones were done with a rainbow of luminous contrasts. This concept of color blending is applied to the Impressionist Landscape technique. Each element in your landscape will be interpreted with several color-dominant and color-related prints. You will be working with literally dozens of fabrics. This isn't as difficult as it may sound because, believe it or not, it's much easier to put fifty fabrics in a quilt than it is to combine five fabrics that are in perfect harmony.

DETAIL OF SUMMER MORNING SKY BY GAI PERRY

Summing up Color Theory

I have never gotten up in the morning and said, "Today I am going to make a quilt with a tetrad color scheme," and I probably never will. On the other hand, a knowledge of color theory will help you select just the right tint of blue or that perfect shade of violet. Being able to knowingly choose a polychromatic set of colors to brighten your quilt, or an achromatic set to tone it down, is truly empowering.

DESIGN TOOLS

I'M NOT GENERALLY A WELL-ORGANIZED PERSON, but before I start a new quilt project I like to have my sewing room tidy and all my equipment lined up and ready to use. My design wall is clean and free of threads, my scissors are sharpened, and there's a new blade in my rotary cutter. Once I start designing, chaos reigns and any sense of order goes out the window, but it feels good to at least start fresh.

Before we get into the "nitty gritty" of fabric selection, let's assemble the necessary tools. You aren't going to need a closet full of trendy gadgets to design an Impressionist Landscape quilt. The list is short and the items are readily available.

- One piece of 100% cotton flannel that measures at least 36″ x 45″ or larger
- One piece of foam-core board that measures 40″ x 48″ or larger (available at craft and art supply stores)
- Sharp pair of fabric cutting scissors
- Rotary cutter and mat
- "See-thru" template plastic
- Scissors to cut the template plastic
- Fabric marking equipment such as a white Chaco-liner®, a white or silver pencil, and a fine-point permanent black pen
- Accurate ruler for cutting and measuring
- Straight pins
- Reducing glass: This tool is just the opposite of a magnifying glass. It allows you to see what your design looks like from a distance even though you're standing right in front of it. Flaws in blending and value areas are apparent when you're looking through the glass.

The following items are not recommended. They will confuse you and perhaps even give false design information.

- Red acrylic value finder   • Any brand of instant camera

Many of the different color areas of an Impressionist Landscape quilt are too subtle to register in a photograph from an instant camera. I know this for a fact because I've ruined a quilt top this way. I kept taking pictures and softening the value areas until the photograph looked good. When the quilt was sewn together, it was nothing but a dull blob of little squares.

MAKING A DESIGN BOARD

Designing an Impressionist Landscape quilt is very much like painting a picture. Similar to working on an artist's easel, the work is done on a vertical surface. All the little squares of fabric (your palette of colors) should be arranged in their proper place before the first stitch is sewn.

An easy and effective method for making a design board is to purchase a piece of foam core that measures at least 40″ x 48″. If you have access to a van, truck, or station wagon, get a stock size piece that measures 40″ x 60″. Splurge and get the half-inch thickness—it won't bend and it will last longer.

Fold the piece of white cotton flannel in half horizontally, and then in half vertically. With an iron, press along the folds. Open the flannel and mark the fold lines with a permanent black pen. Marking the center lines on the flannel will help you to keep the rows of squares straight. Use straight pins to firmly attach the flannel to the board. The squares of fabric will adhere to the flannel without the need for pinning. Lean the design board against a wall or sturdy chair and you're all set to start designing.

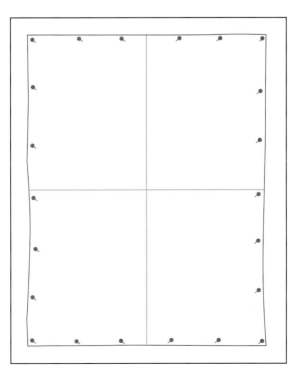

FLANNEL DESIGN BOARD

CUTTING TECHNIQUES

THE ROTARY CUTTER HAS BECOME our best friend…and our worst design enemy. It is so easy to cut several strips from a few fabrics, to get the job done, that we forget the original essence of quiltmaking: gathering a multitude of scraps. A piece from a husband's worn-out shirt, a remnant from a daughter's dress—these unrelated bits of cloth came together to form the extravagantly colored scrap quilts that we revere today. While I'm not asking you to throw away your rotary cutter, I do ask that you use it with a little more restraint. You will have the opportunity to practice that restraint since many of the floral fabrics in your landscape must be cut by hand to insure that an individual flower is centered in each square.

As with any quiltmaking project, accurate templates and precise cutting are important. If your skills are not up to par, hand cutting many of the squares and triangles for these projects will make an expert out of you.

Trace the template patterns, found on pages 125–126, onto the see-thru plastic with a fine point permanent black pen. Cut them out using a blade or paper scissors. Remember to trace the seam allowance onto the templates. This will enable you to see exactly what the squares and triangles of fabric will look like after they are sewn.

Cutting Individual Flowers On Point

Move the 2¼″-square template over your fabric until you can see an individual flower nicely framed within the seam allowance. Mark the fabric with a Chaco-liner®, pencil, or pen and cut the square using fabric scissors (or a rotary cutter and board). Since all the squares will be sewn on point, it is necessary to position the flower so when it is cut, it looks as if it's "growing" toward one of the four points.

Because of this positioning of the flowers, you will frequently be cutting off-grain. Don't worry about grain lines until you start cutting triangles, and then, whenever possible, cut each triangle so that the longest side is on a straight grain.

Right   Wrong

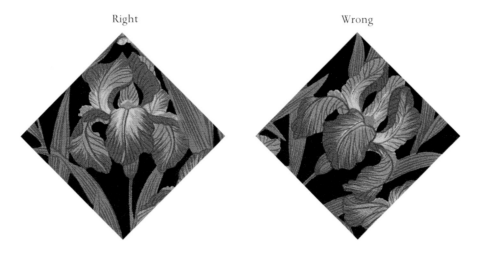

CUTTING INDIVIDUAL FLOWERS ON POINT

Crosswise grain line

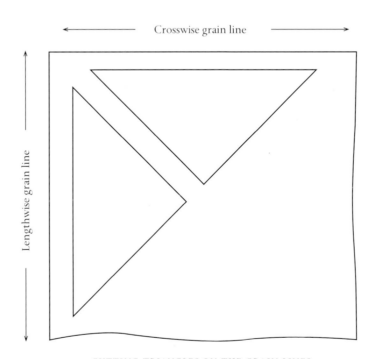

Lengthwise grain line

CUTTING TRIANGLES ON THE GRAIN LINES

Cutting Element Prints and Flowers that Grow in Masses

Most of the fabrics you use to represent elements (sky, water, hills) in your landscape may be cut on the straight of the grain using a rotary cutter. First cut the 2¼″ strips and then cut the strips into squares. Once in a while you may have to cut the 2¼″ strips on a 45° angle to accommodate the direction of a printed texture.

Selvage

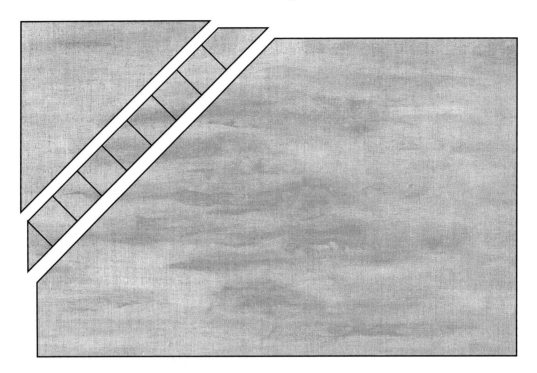

Selvage

CUTTING THE STRIPS ON A 45° ANGLE

ALL ABOUT FABRICS

YOU PROBABLY OWN VERY FEW FABRICS that are appropriate for the Impressionist Landscape technique, so let's have some fun: let's go shopping!

You will be looking at fabrics in an entirely different way than you ever have before. Coordinating an attractive color scheme is not the primary objective. Instead, try to focus on printed fabrics that suggest natural elements like sky, trees, hills, meadows, water, and of course, flowers (all colors and varieties). Flowers are the primary focus of an Impressionist Landscape so the more flower fabrics you can add, the prettier you'll make your quilt.

But before you mortgage the farm to buy fabric, move ahead for a moment and look at the yardage requirements for THE FLOWER GARDEN on page 57. Concentrate on gathering flowers for this first project. After designing the quilt, if you still want to continue, then you can start collecting in earnest!

General Fabric Information

Buy printed fabrics only! No exceptions! Solid colors lack the texture that is necessary for these landscapes.

Look at both sides of a fabric for possible use. Sometimes the reverse side of a fabric will appear softer and more interesting than the front. You will frequently be using both sides of a fabric to help the transition from one color area to another, so look for fabrics that are attractive on both sides.

Print scale is important. Print scale refers to the size of the repeated image. Large scale flowers are repeated at less frequent intervals than small scale flowers. When I suggest using flowers with a similar print scale, I mean using flowers that are all the same size.

Although 100% cotton fabrics are preferable, don't rule out a fabric blend if it is a perfect sky fabric, or if the scale of the flower is just right. Also consider using lightweight designer and upholstery fabrics.

Prewash your fabrics only if you feel the need to do so. I prefer not to wash them because I think that the manufacturer's sizing helps to keep the colors from fading. But you should test for colorfastness and save the fabrics that bleed for other projects.

How much and how many? That's the big question. Naturally, more fabric is better. Isn't that a quilter's commandment? Thou shall buy more, and more, and more! Minimum fabric amounts are suggested, but if you find an exceptionally colorful fabric with printed flowers that are the right scale for both the large and small squares, buy at least two yards.

All the recommended types of flower prints will be discussed in the next section, and those fabrics relating to other landscape elements will be addressed within the appropriate project. It is important to note that all ELEMENT PRINTS should be cut into 2¼″ squares and triangles only. If you cut them larger, they tend to look blocky and too obvious in the finished wall hanging.

PICKING FLOWERS

Flowers, flowers, flowers…big ones, small ones, bright ones, blue ones! They are the reason these Impressionist Landscapes "speak" to us. To start with, you will be delighted to know that the manufacturers of printed floral fabrics have done most of the color work for you. If you are able (with the color theory principles) to put a compatible group of flowers together, your landscape will have built-in contrasts of color, value, and saturation. You can just sit back and accept the applause. So how does one put a compatible group of floral prints together? The following illustrations show the three types of compatibility that need to be considered for a landscape quilt.

1. Flowers that are viewed from the same degree of distance should have a similar print scale.

Right   Wrong

CONSISTENCY OF PRINT SCALE

2. Generally speaking, floral prints in a landscape look better when they are arranged in shaded, toned, tinted or pure groups. Varying degrees of intensity may be used in different areas but the movement from one area to another should be gradual. If you were to put a shaded flower in the middle of a group of tinted flowers, the shaded flower would look like a dark shadow and appear too heavy. A SIMPLE COUNTRY HOUSE on page 117 of the Quilt Gallery illustrates this gradual shift of intensity. Naturally there are exceptions. When you are working toward a contrast of saturation you will have to combine bright flowers with duller ones. The contrast will be successful if you choose flowers that are similar in scale and character. A WILLIAM MORRIS GARDEN on page 118 is a good example of contrast of saturation.

SHADED FLORAL PRINTS

TONED FLORAL PRINTS

TINTED FLORAL PRINTS

PURE FLORAL PRINTS

3. Flowers should have a similar character. Character categories include realistic (flowers that are designed to appear true to life), stylized (flowers that have the look of crewel embroidery or perhaps have an Oriental flair), and painterly floral prints (flowers that look as if an artist had painted them).

REALISTIC FLORAL PRINTS

STYLIZED FLORAL PRINTS

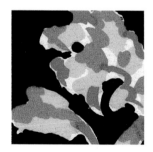   

PAINTERLY FLORAL PRINTS

Examples of Flower Types and Square Size

All the floral prints for the four Impressionist Landscape projects will be cut into either 2¼″ or 4″ squares. For help in selecting the right flowers, make a cardboard viewer that has cut-outs for a 1¾″ and a 3½″ finished square. When you look at a printed flower through the cut-out, you will see exactly what it will look like when it is sewn.

Floral Prints for 2¼″ Squares and Triangles

Most important is the size of an individual flower. An individual flower should fill the entire 1¾″ finished square. The only exception would be flowers that grow in masses (like pansies). Refer to the examples on page 49.

Select floral prints with dark backgrounds only! Black, navy, and dark green are ideal colors for the background; they may be mixed together within each landscape. You may prefer working with lighter background flowers but they often look too dull or faded when combined with the higher contrast of flowers with dark backgrounds.

If you work with the right scale of floral prints, most of the dark backgrounds will disappear when your quilt is sewn together, leaving a lovely blend of brightly-colored flowers. It is possible to make a landscape using all light background fabrics, but it is much more difficult.

Don't focus on a particular color scheme. Instead, choose colors by imagining yourself picking a luxurious mixed bouquet. At this early stage, it's challenging enough to find the right size floral prints without having to worry about color combinations.

All the fabric swatches on the following pages are shown slightly smaller than actual size.

FLORAL PRINTS FOR 2¼″ SQUARES AND TRIANGLES

Floral Prints for 4″ Squares and Triangles

After they are sewn, one 4″ square is equal to four 2¼″ squares. For the larger squares follow the same criteria given for the 2¼″ flower squares; however, now you have the opportunity to focus on more than one flower.

FLORAL PRINTS FOR 4″ SQUARES AND TRIANGLES

Flower-Leaf Transition Prints for 2¼″ Squares

This print is of a relatively small-scale flower and leaf combination. Its function is to fool the eye and to ease the movement from one color and/or value area to another. Use dark backgrounds only. Usually these prints can be rotary cut into 2¼″ strips, and then into 2¼″ squares.

FLOWER-LEAF TRANSITION PRINTS FOR 2¼″ SQUARES

Flowers That Grow in Masses for 2¼" Squares

Many low-growing flowers like pansies, violets, and alyssum cluster together. Usually these prints can be rotary cut.

FLOWERS THAT GROW IN MASSES FOR 2¼" SQUARES

Far-Distance Meadow Flowers #2 for 2¼" Squares ▶

These are even smaller scale floral prints than those of the FAR-DISTANCE MEADOW FLOWERS #1. Use dark or medium-dark backgrounds only. These prints can also be rotary cut.

Far-Distance Meadow Flowers #1 for 2¼" Squares ▶

Choosing the right scale floral prints for the meadow categories can be tricky. Try to find small prints with clusters of multicolored flowers. Use dark backgrounds only. These prints can be rotary cut.

FAR–DISTANCE MEADOW FLOWERS #2 FOR 2¼″ SQUARES

FAR–DISTANCE MEADOW FLOWERS #1 FOR 2¼″ SQUARES

Inappropriate Floral Prints

Small regularly repeating calico prints with a lot of background showing do not work well, nor do floral prints that are too stylized or too playfully rendered.

FLOWER PRINT IS TOO PLAYFUL

LIGHT BACKGROUNDS

TOO MUCH BACKGROUND
SHOWING

PRINT REPEAT IS TOO
REGULAR

PRINT SCALE IS TOO
SMALL

FLOWER PRINT TOO
VAGUE

FLOWER PRINT TOO
STYLIZED

BACKGROUND
INTERFERES WITH
FLOWERS

DESIGN CONCERNS

DESIGNING AN IMPRESSIONIST LANDSCAPE QUILT is not an exact science. I wish I could give you a perfect set of formulas (like the specific measurements for making a quilt block) to guarantee success. Unfortunately it's not possible. Your choice of fabrics, your ability to discern relative values, and your intuitive color sense are the ruling factors in the development of these landscape projects. Let common sense guide you. The bottom line is that you are the person who must be pleased with the final result. If that means making changes in a pattern, or going in another direction, then do it.

The four Impressionist Landscapes projects are presented in order of difficulty. You should start with THE FLOWER GARDEN and then carry the cumulative information with you to each new project.

Use the Master Diagrams for each new project as a guide. You can follow them exactly or try enlarging or changing them. You are limited only by your imagination and the size of your design board.

Design Suggestions

Creating a dazzling arrangement of flowers is the primary goal of an Impressionist Landscape quilter. You want to give the viewer an irresistible sensation of color and contrast. Here are some design suggestions that you can apply to all four of the Impressionist Landscape projects.

• Always work in good light and, if possible, natural daylight. If you are a night person, be consistent about working on the project during the evening hours only. Colors change dramatically in night lighting.

• Gradually, as you work with the flower squares, your ability to blend a greater variety of colors and fabrics will grow. Floral prints that looked at first like they wouldn't work might later blend perfectly when there are more squares on your design board.

• If some of the squares in a particular area don't please you, try not to dwell on them. Leave them in place, for the time being, and continue designing. You can do revisions later when your landscape is further along and you have a better understanding of what you want it to look like.

• Try not to design for more than five or six consecutive hours. After that, you'll become obsessive and end up making mistakes. (You're laughing now, but wait until you start—it's very addictive!)

• If you have trouble following a Master Diagram, try this: Position a square of fabric on the design board and then mark, or shade in, the corresponding square on the Master Diagram for reference.

• Make an effort to keep the design rows straight while you work; it will make it much easier to sew the rows together later on.

• If a new flower or element print is introduced and it looks too bright, don't immediately discard it; flip the fabric over to the reverse side and try it again.

• Every floral fabric that is introduced in the design should be repeated in at least two other squares. Using just one square from a fabric will make it stand out; it will look out of place.

• Don't spend fifteen minutes staring at a fabric wondering if it will work. It only takes a few seconds to cut out a square and try it!

• Keep referring to the project quilt for ideas and placement of the squares. One of the best ways to learn a new technique is to copy the example as closely as possible. Creativity and individuality can come later, when you've mastered the technique.

• The reducing glass should be a constant companion. Keep using it to check the blending of value and color from one area to another.

• Before sewing your landscape, live with it for awhile. Look at it during different times of day and keep trying to improve it.

• It's never too late to change a square. Even after the quilt top is sewn, you can still pick out any offending squares and replace them. I do it all the time.

THE FLOWER GARDEN, 1992, 32″ X 34″, GAI PERRY

THE FLOWER GARDEN

THE FLOWER GARDEN WALL HANGING is an uncomplicated view of a flower bed. There is a grassy area in the foreground and a suggestion of a hedge, or leafy area, in the background. There is no need to establish distance or work toward the horizon because the design places the viewer directly in front of the flower bed.

Study the color photograph of THE FLOWER GARDEN and you will notice that the motion of the flowers is toward the right corner. This slight angle gives the flower bed a nice feeling of movement. This movement is balanced by a larger dark green area in the upper left corner and a larger light green area in the lower right corner.

THE FLOWER GARDEN has three distinct value areas. The leafy foliage area at the top is the darkest value. The flowers, as a whole, read as the medium value and the grassy foreground is the lightest value. The cool colors of the grass and foliage contrast with the warm colors of the flower bed. You can establish another attractive contrast within the floral area by blending warm-colored flowers (reds, yellows, and oranges) with cool-colored flowers (purples, violets, and blues).

To get into the mood to purchase fabrics for this wall hanging, visualize a breathtakingly beautiful flower bed, where each bloom is precisely placed for maximum color effect. Remember, since you are standing directly in front of the flower bed you don't need to establish distance and you can concentrate on the natural arrangement of the flowers.

Start the design near the grassy area with low-growing border flowers such as pansies or violets. Above these, you might add some daffodils and iris, or maybe some tulips. Then perhaps add some roses, daisies, and chrysanthemums. Finally, a few tall flowers like hollyhocks or sunflowers would look appropriate. Adding fresh green grass in the foreground and dark green foliage in the background completes the picture. If you aren't a gardener, you can invoke your artistic license. This gives you permission to arrange the flowers any way you choose without worrying about what is correct. Remember, this is art!

For this first project, stay away from a controlled color scheme. It's too limiting unless you've built up an extensive collection of floral fabrics. Instead, imagine that you're picking a mixed bouquet; let the "flowers" in the fabric, with all their built-in contrasts, do the color work for you.

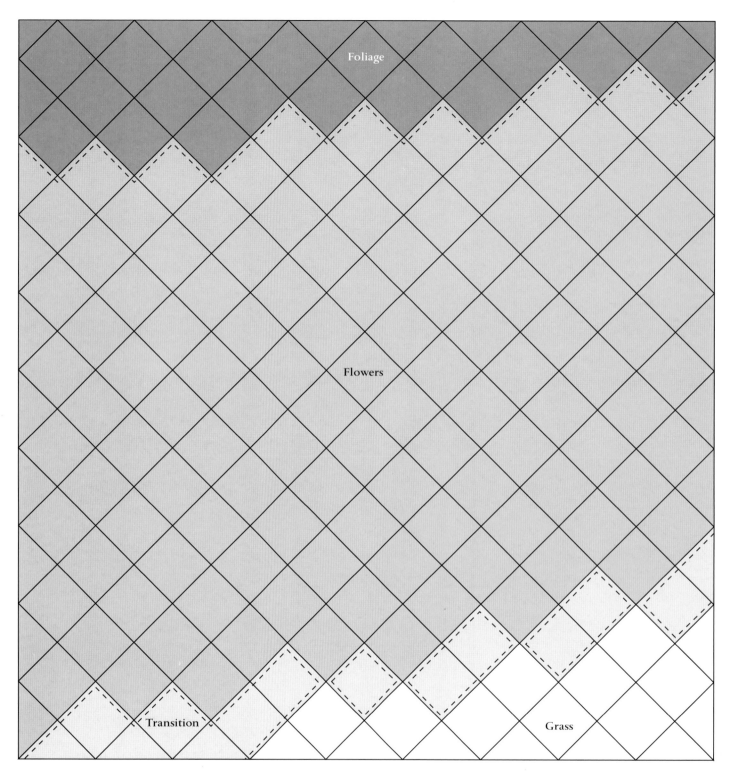

Foliage

Flowers

Transition

Grass

MASTER DIAGRAM FOR THE FLOWER GARDEN

56

Flower Prints

Select floral fabrics that have a similar character. A contemporary tulip won't fit into a bed of old-fashioned roses. They look too different. Refer to the examples on page 44.

THE FLOWER GARDEN only uses the 2¼″ squares and triangles. Select a group of flower fabrics that have the same scale as FLORAL PRINTS FOR 2¼″ SQUARES shown on page 46. The minimum yardage amounts are half-yard cuts each of six different fabrics.

TRANSITION PRINTS: The transition print creates the graceful movement from the border flowers to the grassy areas. This print should be a small flower-leaf combination fabric. Refer to FLOWER-LEAF TRANSITION PRINTS FOR 2¼″ SQUARES on page 48 for examples. The leaves should be a medium to light green color. You will need an eighth of a yard of one fabric.

GRASS PRINTS: Use two or three of the light, lighter, and lightest value tone-on-tone prints. You will need an eighth-yard cut of each. Wait to purchase these fabrics until you've finished designing the flower bed.

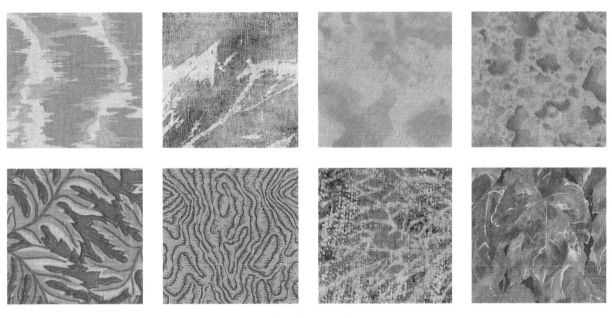

GRASS PRINTS

FOLIAGE PRINTS: Use three or four dark green color-dominant and tone-on-tone prints. Refer to definitions on page 17. You will need eighth-yard cuts of each. The print scale and value of these fabrics should be similar but, again, wait to purchase these until you've finished designing the flower bed.

FOLIAGE PRINTS

Begin the Design

You now have most of the basic information that's necessary to design your flower garden. Remember, creativity is a "hands on" trial and error struggle. As you practice, you will educate your eye to know what looks good and what needs changing. Learn to trust your instincts! If you have to ask yourself if a particular floral print looks appropriate, it probably doesn't.

Start by cutting two or three 2¼″ squares from each of your selected flower fabrics. In the middle section of your design board, arrange the squares on point (with one square touching the next). This is a temporary design arrangement to allow you to become familiar with the interaction of your flower prints.

TEMPORARY DESIGN ARRANGEMENT

To decide whether or not the flowers look like they belong in the same garden, ask yourself the following questions:

1. Do some of the flower squares stand out because they look too bright (saturated), too dull, or too gray?

2. Does the design look as if there are two different flower gardens in the works? If so, you need to decide which direction to pursue and then eliminate the flowers that don't blend, and add others.

3. Does the character of the flowers appear similar?

4. Is the scale and relationship of the flowers believable?

When you have several floral prints that look good together, refer to the Master Diagram and start "planting" your garden.

Step One: Cut ten 2¼″ squares and four 2¼″ triangles from the transition print. Arrange them according to the Master Diagram. This arrangement establishes the upward movement of the flowers and indicates the width of the flower bed. If, at any point, you are not satisfied with the way your transition print blends into the border flowers, or later into the grass, choose another fabric.

Step Two: Continue cutting 2¼″ squares from your flower fabrics and gradually work toward the dark green foliage at the top. Refer to the Master Diagram and quilt photograph for inspiration and flower positions. Keep in mind that, in real life, flowers are usually planted in "groupings" rather than individually. If any of the floral prints have some attractive leaves, you might include a few squares of just leaves, here and there, for a touch of green contrast.

Step Three: When all the flower squares and triangles are in place (don't worry about the garden looking perfect just yet), add the grass and dark green foliage.

Look at the dominant shades of green in the leaves of the flower squares and choose lighter values for the grass. An example is if the leaves of the flowers appear to be a gray-green, choose lighter gray-green colors for the grass. This rule applies to the foliage as well, but here, choose darker values of the gray-green.

Grass—Cut the appropriate number of squares and triangles. Refer to the Master Diagram for placement. Place the darkest of the light green prints next to the transition print; place the lightest green toward the outer edge. It is possible to use just one fabric by making the front of the fabric the darker value and the reverse side the lighter value.

Foliage—Cut several squares from each of your selected fabrics and place them randomly across the top. There is no formula here. You will have to decide when it looks right. A hint: The flowers should blend into the foliage without a lot of obvious sawtooth points. Cut the top row of flower squares so more of the dark background shows. The dark background will help the flowers ease into the foliage. Finally, add the foliage triangles to finish the design.

Step Four: Now that all the squares and triangles are in place, it's time to "fine tune." Keep changing and rearranging until you are convinced you can't make it any better. The sewing instructions begin on page 84.

Try switching the light and dark value positions. Make the grass dark and the foliage light.

Delete the foliage and instead add a sky.

If you have lots of flower prints, and are feeling brave, enlarge the landscape and include some of the 4" flower squares. Place them toward the top of the flower bed to represent taller flowers.

NOTES:

COUNTRY MEADOWS, 1995, 34″ X 42″, GAI PERRY

COUNTRY MEADOWS

COUNTRY MEADOWS FEATURES A VOLUPTUOUS flowering meadow backed by distant hills and a softly impressionistic sky. Between the meadow and the hills there is one row of green squares to suggest a stand of trees. This single row of green squares was put in to mark the horizon line and to act as a focal point. It also helps blend the meadow into the hills.

This landscape has three distinct value areas. The sky is the lightest value, the flowering meadow is the medium value, and the hills are the darkest value. The color scheme is polychromatic and there is a strong contrast of warm-cool colors.

Begin by designing the meadow foreground and gradually work toward the sky area. I'll explain the element fabric choices for each of the areas as we reach them, so if you wait until then to purchase the fabrics you'll have a much better feel of what to buy.

Both the 2¼″ and 4″ squares and triangles (plus two corner triangles) will be used for this project.

Meadow Flowers

All the flower fabrics in the meadow, no matter what the print scale, should have the same color assortment. In other words, the tiny flowers at the back of the meadow should give the illusion of the foreground flowers, but from a greater distance.

LARGE FOREGROUND FLOWERS: Select three or four compatible fabrics. You'll need at least a half yard of each. Refer to FLORAL PRINTS FOR 4″ SQUARES on page 47 for examples.

MID-DISTANCE FLOWERS: Select five or six floral fabrics that reflect the same colors found in the larger squares, but are smaller in print scale. Refer to FLORAL PRINTS FOR 2¼″ SQUARES on page 46 for examples. You'll need half yard cuts of each. Note: usually you can find some of the mid-distance flowers grouped within the larger scale flower prints.

FAR-DISTANCE MEADOW FLOWERS #1: You will need three or four different prints of the same color family as above. Refer to examples on page 50. You'll need a quarter yard of each.

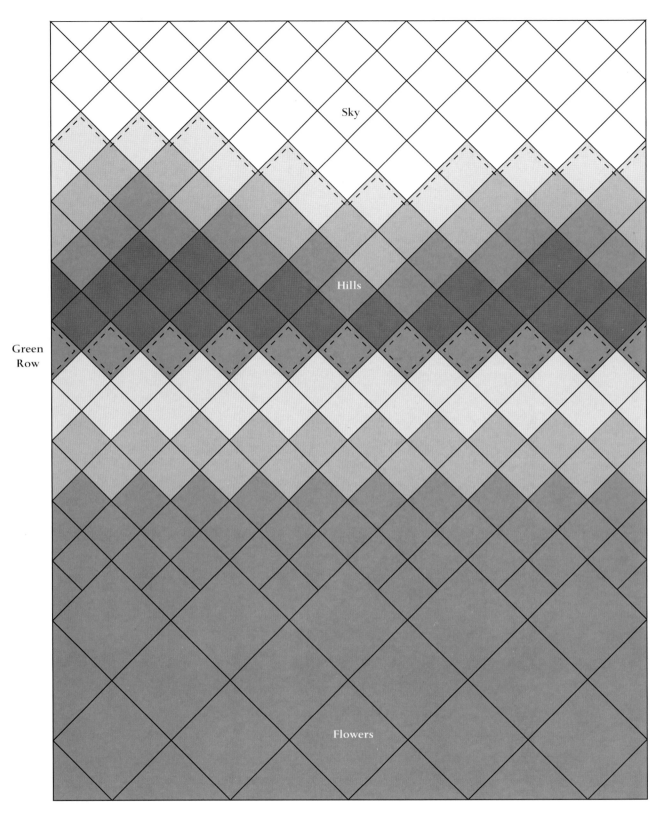

Sky

Hills

Green
Row

Flowers

MASTER DIAGRAM FOR COUNTRY MEADOWS

FAR-DISTANCE MEADOW FLOWERS #2: Purchase one or two small-scale flower prints in the same color groups as the larger flowers. Refer to page 50 for examples. Buy eighth-yard cuts of each. Reminder: little regularly repeating calicos, with lots of background showing, are inappropriate.

Begin the Design

Step One: Select the template square that measures 4″ and cut fourteen large flower squares for the foreground. Refer to the Master Diagram for placement. Try not to cut the same flower twice in exactly the same way. Even though all the flowers are cut to grow skyward, they can also be cut to angle slightly to the left or right to give them a different look. Each time you cut a new square, place it on the lower section of your design board and try to make it blend with the other flowers. Remember to apply what you learned in the previous landscape project about combining flowers with a similar character. You may end up cutting several extra squares before getting the right balance of color and flower compatibility.

When you have a pleasing arrangement, add the side and corner triangles.

PLACEMENT OF LARGE SQUARES AND TRIANGLES

Until they are sewn, each large square takes up less physical space than four smaller squares. This section must be "opened up" so the rest of the design, which consists of small squares only, will fit properly. Refer to example on the following page and place this section at the bottom of the design board.

"OPENED UP" SECTION OF LOWER MEADOW

Step Two: The next few rows will consist of mid-distance flowers. Follow the Master Diagram for placement. Squares in this section consist of individual flowers, or two or three flowers per square.

Step Three: Now the flower scale gets progressively smaller and lighter in value. Use FAR-DISTANCE MEADOW FLOWERS #1, and then FAR-DISTANCE MEADOW FLOWERS # 2, to reach the row of green squares. Use the reverse sides of your flower prints to help with the illusion of distance. Keep referring to the Master Diagram and the COUNTRY MEADOWS quilt for placement and design ideas.

When all the meadow squares are filled in, use the reducing glass to check for design errors. When you look through the glass you should see a smooth transition from the foreground of the meadow to the background. Wherever a flower square pops out, it is because the print scale is wrong or the color is too intense or too light; change it to make a better blend.

Green Row

Step Four: This one is easy! Find two or three medium-value green tone-on-tone prints that are similar in pattern scale. You will need eighth-yard cuts of each. The print pattern should not be sharp or distinct because you want to project a sense of distance. Choose shades of green that are similar to the dominant color of the leaves in the meadow. Refer to the GREEN ROW PRINTS below for examples. Cut a total of nine squares and two triangles from these fabrics and place them randomly across the design board in the appropriate position. Refer to the Master Diagram for placement.

GREEN ROW PRINTS

Hills and Sky

The hill and sky fabrics are chosen at the same time because they are dependent on each other. *Whatever color is chosen for the sky must be reflected in the hills by darker values of the same color.*

FOR THE SKY: You will need only one sky fabric so choose something that you really like. You'll need a half-yard cut. Try a dramatic sunset tie-dyed fabric, a bright blue textured fabric, or a pink marbleized fabric. Just about any sky color is possible. Refer to the SKY PRINTS below for examples.

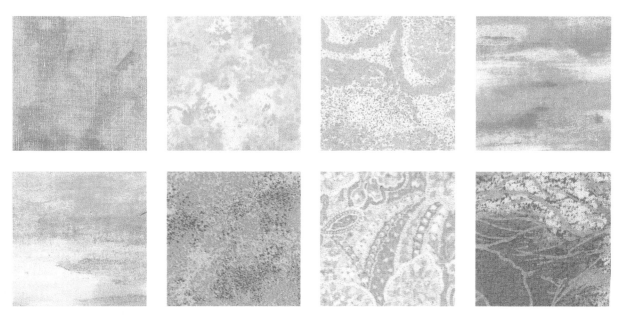

SKY PRINTS

FOR THE HILLS: Look for four color-dominant and color-related prints plus one print that will be used to transition into the sky. The prints should be value-graded from medium dark to medium light. You'll need quarter-yard cuts of each. Refer to the VALUE-GRADED HILL PRINTS below for examples.

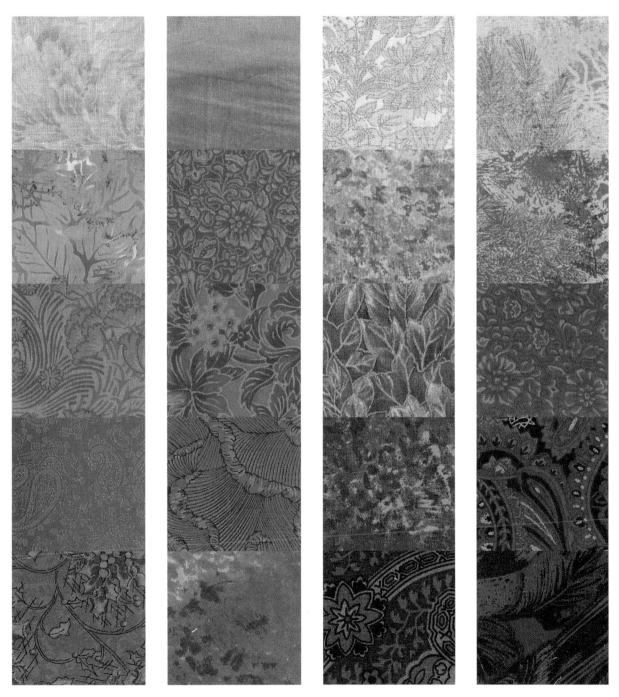

VALUE-GRADED HILL PRINTS

Step Five: The first two rows of the hills, above the green row, are worked with the two darkest prints; they are used interchangeably. Continue to use these same two prints to define the line of the hills. Refer to the EXPLODED VIEW OF HILL CONSTRUCTION diagram as a guide. (Continue placing the squares point to point; the diagram is for reference only.)

EXPLODED VIEW OF HILL CONSTRUCTION

Each successively lighter value fabric, including the transition print, should be cut into enough squares to make one complete row across the line of hills. Place them on the design board in the order indicated on the Master Diagram and continue using the EXPLODED VIEW OF HILL CONSTRUCTION example as a guide.

Step Six: Cut enough squares and side triangles to complete the sky. Refer to the Master Diagram for placement.

Step Seven: Critique your work. Look at it through the reducing glass. Ideally, each section should "melt" into the next. If the hill fabrics are chosen correctly, it should be difficult to tell where the hills stop and the sky begins.

Interesting phenomena: The color selected for the sky will emphasize, and bring out, all the meadow flowers that are in the same color family. The whole meadow will glow with the reflected color of the sky.

Try using a monochromatic color scheme: a field of sunflowers with golden hills and a buttermilk sky.

Make rugged mountain peaks instead of vague hills; eliminate the "transition to sky" fabric so the mountains are clearly defined.

NOTES:

THE GARDEN PATH, 1994, 35" X 43", GAI PERRY

THE GARDEN PATH

THE GARDEN PATH IS REMINISCENT OF an opulent Victorian garden. A path meanders toward the rear of the garden and there is a suggestion of bushes and dense green foliage that transition into sky.

This project introduces a path as its focal point. The path is a light value and it sweeps toward the sky with a graceful diagonal movement. "Transition" is the key to making this landscape work. Careful thought must be given to the relationship of the path fabric and the transitional floral fabric that lines the path. They should blend into each other without sharply defined edges. Create this illusion by using both fabrics first on the reverse side and then again on the front side.

A combination of 2¼″ and 4″ squares and triangles are used to establish the foreground flowers. Small squares and triangles will be used to interpret other elements.

MASTER DIAGRAM FOR THE GARDEN PATH

This Master Diagram was altered slightly so the quilt will fit on your design board.

Begin the Design

Step One: Placement of the path. Select a quarter yard of one path fabric. Choose an airy floral print, in a fairly light value, to give the impression of a sun-filtered walk way. Refer to PATH PRINTS for ideas. Use the reverse side of the fabric through the middle of the path. Use the front of the fabric along both sides of the path.

Rotary cut the appropriate amount of path squares and then place them on the design board in the order indicated on the Master Diagram. Note the center square on the Master Diagram marked with an x. Put the corresponding square of path fabric in the exact center of your design board where the horizontal and vertical lines intersect. (If you don't do this, your design will probably flow off the edge of the flannel board.) Add the three triangles along the left edge and the two triangles at the top of the path.

Right side

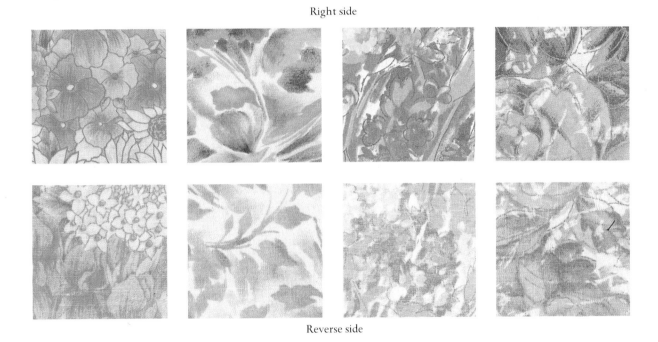

Reverse side

PATH PRINTS

Step Two: The transition flower-leaf print should blend smoothly into the path so there is a graceful movement of the path into the flower areas. Select one print that has the same colors as the path print, but in slightly darker values. One quarter of a yard of this fabric will be enough. Refer to FLOWER-LEAF TRANSITION PRINTS FOR $2\frac{1}{4}''$ SQUARES on page 48 for examples.

Rotary cut the transition squares and position them along both sides of the path. Wherever a transition print square touches a path print square, use the reverse side of the fabric. Use the transition fabric on the front side as it moves into the flower areas. Add the appropriate number of triangles.

Flower Prints

Step Three: By now you should be finding it easier to pick a compatible group of flowers, so this time, the decision of how much and how many is up to you.

Look at the different flower areas in the Master Diagram and select some FLORAL PRINTS FOR 2¼″ AND 4″ SQUARES for the right side of the foreground. These flowers must be cut with templates. Choose a group of FAR-DISTANCE MEADOW FLOWERS #1 for the rear section of the garden. Note that in THE GARDEN PATH quilt these flowers are in darker values than the foreground flowers. Look for a print that resembles a flowering hedge to put along the back of the garden. The lighter value flowers will be effective against the dark green foliage above them.

It is advisable to have all the flower spaces filled in before starting the foliage and sky sections. Don't fuss with the flowers too much at this point, because after the dark greens are added, the flowers will look brighter and livelier. You may not have to do as much changing as you thought.

Foliage and Sky

Step Four: Choose one soft-looking leaf print in a medium value to put at the top of the path. Use the front side of the fabric where it touches the path. Use the reverse side to blend into the sky. Refer to LEAF PRINTS for ideas. Buy an eighth of a yard. Refer to the Master Diagram for placement.

LEAF PRINTS

Step Five: Select an eighth of a yard of one sky fabric in a lighter color and value than the leaf print. Refer to SKY PRINTS in the previous landscape project for examples. Refer to the Master Diagram for placement of sky squares and triangles.

Step Six: Find three or four dominant-color and color-related prints for the foliage area. They should also be value-graded from light to dark. Buy eighth-yard cuts of each. Refer to the VALUE-GRADED FOLIAGE PRINTS below for examples. Place the lightest value foliage print on both sides of the sky. Ideally, this print should blend so nicely that it becomes hard to tell where the sky ends and the foliage starts. Move outward, on both sides, using gradually darker values. (Note the vertical positioning of each of these value-graded fabrics.) Refer to the Master Diagram for placement.

Leaf print for top of path

Right side   Reverse side   Lightest

Darkest

VALUE-GRADED FOLIAGE PRINTS

Step Seven: Fine tune your design. Use the reducing glass to spot errors. Make sure that the path is still the main focus.

BREAK-AWAY IDEAS

Turn the path into a flowing stream.

Put a gate at the back of the path instead of the leaf print. Look at the MONET'S GARDEN quilt on page 97 for an example.

Try working with a complementary color scheme.

Experiment with some of the other template pattern sizes. The rectangular shape is perfect for flowers with stems and leaves.

THE WATERFALL, 1994, 35″ X 41″, GAI PERRY

$\mathcal{T}$HE WATERFALL

THE WATERFALL IS MORE ABSTRACT than the other three landscape projects because the different elements are suggested rather than clearly defined. The waterfall cascades diagonally down and across the surface of the picture. The lightness of the water is in startling contrast to the dark foliage areas on either side. A hint of sunlight peaks through the greenery in the upper right corner; it's balanced by a sprinkling of light flowers in the lower left corner. Think of this project as a graduation exercise. It is going to be very easy or very difficult depending on how skillfully you select the fabrics.

For the first time, you will be in control of the color scheme and you must decide what set of analogous colors you want to work with. THE WATERFALL quilt is designed with light, medium, and dark values of blue and green. There are touches of turquoise, deep violet, and lavender. The landscape colors are very cool and satisfying. You can choose colors that project an entirely different atmosphere. How about a Hawaiian waterfall surrounded by radiant passion flowers, and maybe a volcano in the background…or perhaps, a jungle waterfall with exotic birds and flowers?

THE WATERFALL quilt uses only the 2¼″ square and triangle templates but you have the option of including any of the larger sizes if they will contribute to a better design.

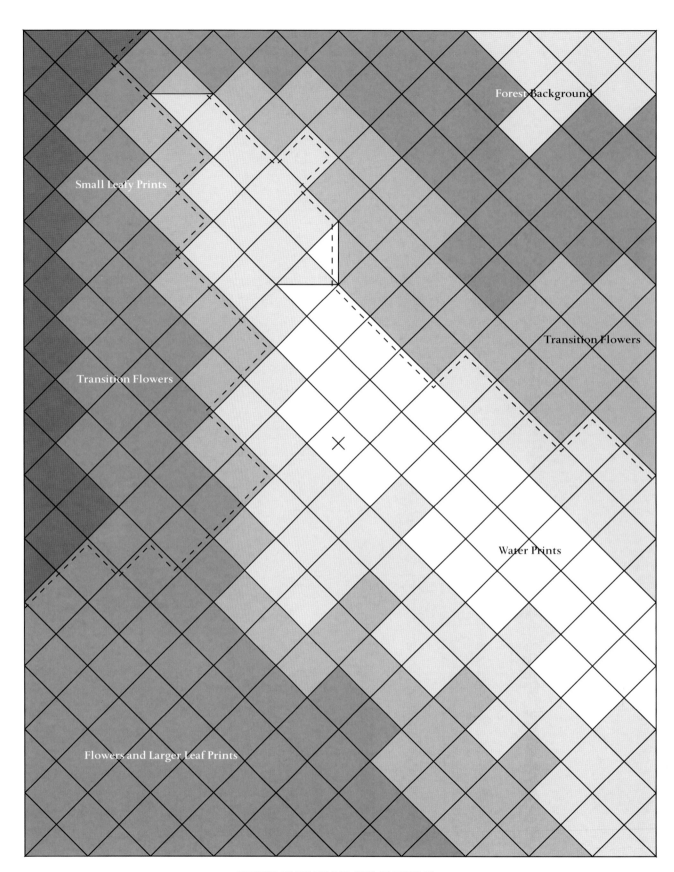

Forest Background

Small Leafy Prints

Transition Flowers

Transition Flowers

Water Prints

Flowers and Larger Leaf Prints

MASTER DIAGRAM FOR THE WATERFALL

The Master Diagram was altered slightly so this quilt can fit your design board.

Begin the Design

Step One: Define the waterfall. When you purchase fabrics for the waterfall, you will be looking for prints that feel liquid and suggest movement or "foaminess." Visualize the water in an impressionistic painting. It isn't painted with one color but rather a combination of several colors. Look for light value fabrics that are highlighted with pastel tints.

It is better to buy lesser amounts of more fabrics in order to get a greater variety of textures to choose from; this rule applies to all the fabrics purchased for this landscape.

Rotary cut 2¼″ squares from several water fabrics. Refer to the WATER PRINTS below for examples. Put the lighter value water fabrics down the center of the waterfall and along the upper right side. Put the darker value water fabrics along the edges of the waterfall so there is a gradual blending into the flower and leafy areas. Refer to the Master Diagram for placement. Again, place the water square with the corresponding x in the center of your design board. Add the appropriate number of water triangles.

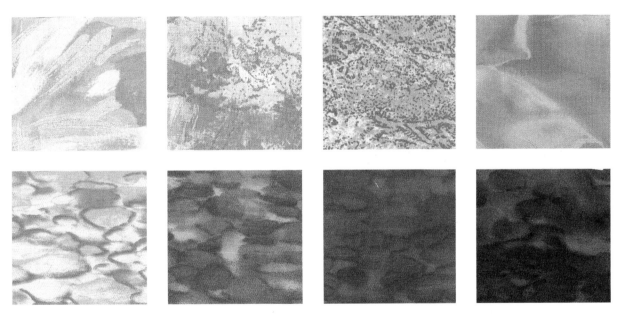

WATER PRINTS

When all the waterfall squares are in place, start cutting squares from the following types of prints. How much and how many are not specified. You will have to decide.

Forest Background Prints

A group of color-related prints that suggest a vague, leafy kind of background. Use medium-dark values. Try to find one print in this group that looks like sunlight shining through trees.

 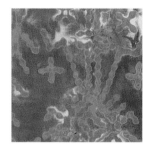  

FOREST BACKGROUND PRINTS

Small-Scale Leafy Prints

You will need two or three small-scale leafy prints in medium to dark values.

SMALL-SCALE LEAFY PRINTS

Individual Flower and Leaf Prints

You will need three or four floral prints. Refer to FLORAL PRINTS FOR 2¼" SQUARES on page 46. You will also need one or two leaf prints. Refer to LEAF PRINTS on page 76.

Transition Prints

Find two or three prints that have small flowers and leaves on them. Refer to FLOWER-LEAF TRANSITION PRINTS FOR 2¼" SQUARES on page 48.

Step Two: Now you're on your own! Study THE WATERFALL quilt and the Master Diagram to familiarize yourself with the different areas. Begin at the top of the quilt and fill in the forest background section on the right side and then the small leafy prints on the left side. Work down to the transition prints, which are used on both sides of the waterfall, and then into the individual flower and leaf prints. Always use the lightest value prints next to the water.

Step Three: Fine tune the design. Use the reducing glass to determine whether the different areas are blending together nicely. Does the water have movement and is it believable? Does it blend into the greenery and foliage on the left side and on the bottom half of the right side?

BREAK-AWAY IDEAS

Put a sky at the top of the waterfall.

Use oversized flowers in the lower left corner and incorporate different sized templates.

Suggest a rocky path along the base of the waterfall.

ASSEMBLING THE LANDSCAPE

I WISH I HAD LEARNED TO SEW when I was young. Unfortunately, I wasn't raised in a family of quiltmakers, nor did I sit at my mother's knee and watch her agile fingers stitch the latest family heirloom. Well…I did sit at her knee once. I watched her sew a button to my father's shirt and simultaneously, to her skirt. Though I was impressed I don't think this single act qualifies as a "heritage."

The bottom line to this story is that when I began designing quilts, sewing was a mystery that had to be unraveled and practiced. If you are a beginning quilter, take heart: Putting an Impressionist Landscape together requires very few sewing skills. If I can do it, so can you!

Equipment

- Sewing machine
- Medium gray 100% cotton sewing machine thread
- Scissors
- Pins
- Seam ripper

PROBLEM: Your design board is covered with hundreds of little squares and triangles that need to be sewn into diagonal strips. (Preferably in the same arrangement that you worked so hard to achieve.)

SOLUTION: Because I was continually having trouble sewing the squares into the correct order, I invented my "no-brainer" method of construction. Follow the diagrams! Once you get into the sewing rhythm it moves quickly and is failure proof.

METHOD: My method for joining squares and triangles works for rows where there are *three or more* squares. You are going to sew the squares and triangles into diagonal strips using a ¼″ seam allowance. Begin sewing at the lower left hand corner of the design and work toward the upper right hand corner. Refer to the sewing diagram.

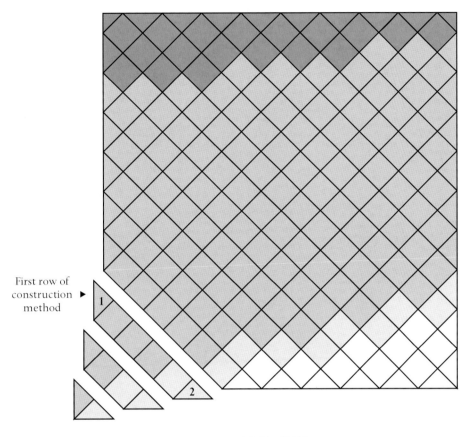

First row of
construction
method ▶

Step One: Starting with the first row of the construction method, sew the upper edge triangle (1) to the square sitting diagonally below it. With the pressure foot still down, sew a few more stitches and leave the unit in the machine.

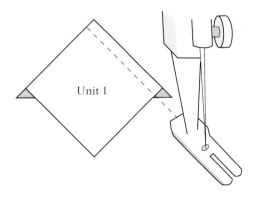

Unit 1

STEP ONE

Step Two: From the same row, pick up the lower edge triangle (2) plus the square sitting diagonally above it and sew them together. With the pressure foot still down, sew a few more stitches and then leave this unit in the machine. With your scissors, detach Unit 1.

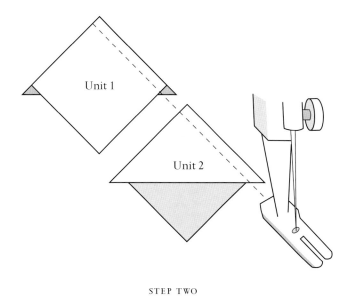

STEP TWO

Step Three: Move back to the top of the row and pick up the next square in the sequence. Sew it to Unit 1. With the pressure foot still down, sew a few more stitches and then leave this unit in the machine. With your scissors, detach Unit 2.

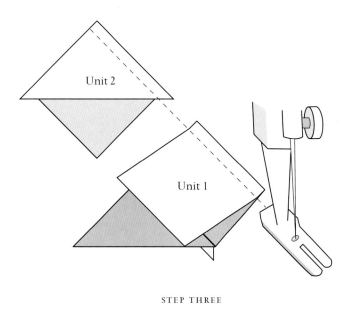

STEP THREE

Step Four: Move down to the lower end of the row and pick up the next square in the sequence. Sew it to Unit 2. With the pressure foot still down, sew a few more stitches and then leave this unit in the machine.

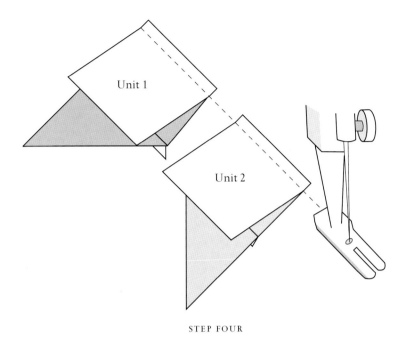

STEP FOUR

Step Five: Continue sewing in this manner until all the squares in the row are joined to the first or second units. Sew the two units together and pin the resulting strip onto the design board in the correct position.

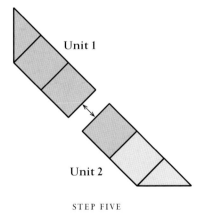

STEP FIVE

The beauty of this method will become obvious to you as you continue joining the squares to the first and second units. The color areas at either end of the row will be so different that you will have no trouble figuring out which square comes next. If you lose your concentration and sew a square to the wrong unit, it will be immediately obvious because the colors won't blend and the square will look out of place.

In rows where there are one or more large squares, two single rows must be joined together before adding them to the larger squares.

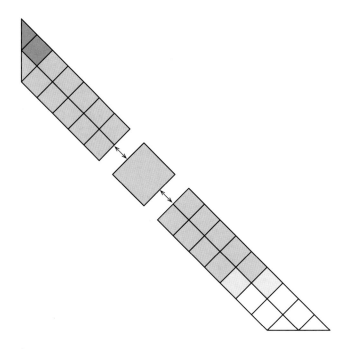

JOINING LARGE SQUARES

Joining the Rows and Pressing

Press the seam allowances for each row in one direction only and alternate the direction from row to row. An example is if the first row is pressed toward the left, press the second row toward the right, and the third row again to the left.

To join the individual rows, start in the lower left-hand corner. Pin the first row to the second row at the opposing seam allowances. Sew the two rows together. Continue joining the rows in this manner. Press all the seam allowances in the same direction, either up or down.

Borders

THE BORDER SHOULD ACT LIKE A FRAME: complement but not overpower the design. Select a simple tone-on-tone print (generally in a cool color) that will contrast with, and enhance, the colors in the landscape. It's difficult to pick out just the right border print because there are so many likely candidates. I usually take my sewn landscape to a fabric store and lay it across several potential border prints until I find one that looks absolutely wonderful. Refer to the examples of appropriate border fabrics on the following page.

Use a thin strip of a white, cream, or pastel solid to separate the landscape from the outer border. It acts like a mat and gives the picture more definition. Occasionally, I add a narrow middle border to give an extra touch of color. If the outer border is a cool color, select a warm color for the middle border.

The borders can have straight or mitered corners. If you prefer to miter the corners, make sure to cut the strips the full length of the quilt plus double the finished border width (plus an extra two or three inches).

The following border measurements are optional and can be changed according to personal taste:

Cut four 1½″-wide strips for the inner border.

Cut four 4½″-wide strips for the outer border.

Cut four ⅞″-wide strips for the optional middle border.

Join the border strips to the four sides of the quilt. If it is your intention to miter the corners, and you are unfamiliar with this procedure, or with any of the sewing procedures in this section, consult one of the many basic sewing skill books that are readily available. My recommended reading list is on page 127.

QUILTING AND FINISHING

WHEN MY FIRST IMPRESSIONIST LANDSCAPE was ready to quilt, I gave a great deal of thought to the pattern. Should my landscape have free-flowing surface stitches? Perhaps some wind currents might be a nice touch. Should some of the flowers be outlined, or even padded, to make them come forward? The conclusion I reached was that I would treat the quilt like a painting and give it a subtle texture, similar to that of a linen canvas.

I decided to quilt the borders with a series of parallel lines. Using a little imagination, these lines suggest an ornately beveled frame. But this is just one quilting solution. There are certainly many patterns that would be equally attractive. I invite your creativity in this area.

Baste your landscape to a good-quality 100% cotton backing. I prefer a radial basting technique because I think it is more appropriate for lap quilting. The back will have less tendency to bunch up.

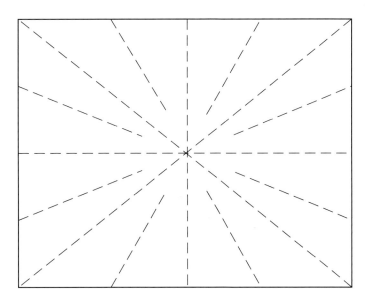

RADIAL BASTING PATTERN

◄ APPROPRIATE BORDER FABRICS

Quilt your landscape by hand or machine, using your own pattern or the one suggested in the QUILTING DIAGRAM.

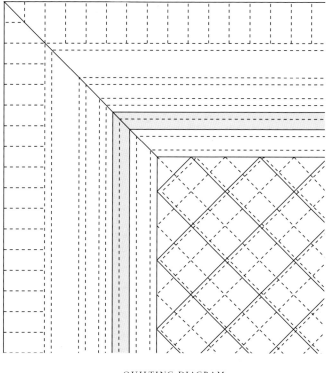

QUILTING DIAGRAM
(Shaded area is the optional middle border.)

FOR HAND QUILTING: The finished landscape should look smooth and flat. Both Mountain Mist Quilt Light® and Fairfield Low-loft® batting are good choices.

Since the quilting pattern is designed for overall texture without being obvious, it is advisable to change the color of your quilting thread to match the different areas. A medium green thread seems to work the best in all the flower areas. Use your favorite brand of quilting thread.

FOR MACHINE QUILTING: Use the thin cotton batting of your choice, and a clear filament thread for quilting. Quilt a diagonal grid along the seam lines only. Omit the quilting stitches through the center of each square.

BLOCKING THE LANDSCAPE: When the quilting is complete, set the landscape on your ironing board. Adjust the iron for a medium-warm, synthetic setting. *Carefully press the front of the quilt using a gentle flow of steam. This procedure is like blocking a sweater; it gives the quilt a beautifully finished look.

Do NOT use a hot iron or your synthetic batting will melt!

Binding

The binding fabric should match the outer border. Measure the length and width of the quilt and then cut four 2¼″ strips to the appropriate length. Fold the strips in half and press. Using a ¼″ seam allowance, machine stitch the raw edges of the strips to the front of the quilt. Fold over and hand stitch to the back.

Finishing Suggestions

Make a sleeve to hang your quilt by cutting a 9″ strip of the backing fabric to the same width of your landscape. Hem both the ends. Fold the strip in half and machine stitch it together to form a tube. Sew the sleeve to the top edge of the quilt back.

Sign your work of art! If the backing fabric is a light enough color, I like to write my label information directly onto the quilt using a permanent pen. If the backing fabric is too dark, make a cloth label of unbleached muslin. The information should include your name, the name of the quilt, the date, the size of the quilt, the materials used, and the geographic location of your home.

THE QUILT GALLERY

IT'S THRILLING FOR ME TO SEE my Impressionist Landscape quilts in print! I have the unique opportunity to view them as a "body of work" to analyze what areas are successful and what areas could be improved. I don't think we should ever allow ourselves to be completely satisfied with our quiltmaking skills. When that happens, we become locked in a status quo environment.

"Birthing" a quilt is a pleasure-pain experience for me. When I'm designing, hours seem like minutes and before I know it, the day has slipped by and I haven't dealt with the breakfast dishes or figured out what to cook for the evening meal. (Luckily, I have a delightful husband who takes me out to dinner when I'm on a creative binge.) I love the focused intensity that goes into making these landscape quilts. The experience has been so intimate that sometimes I felt as if I really was an Impressionist, and the squares of fabrics, my paint.

I hand quilted all of the landscape quilts, except for SUNRISE ON TURQUOISE POND and A SIMPLE COUNTRY HOUSE. These were machine quilted by my friend Margaret Gair. I generally quilt for an hour or two each evening after all my chores are done, just like the pioneer women—but I have good lighting, a soft-upholstered couch, a color television, and a refrigerator filled with tasty snacks. Alas! Woman's work is never done.

The Quilt Gallery is arranged in chronological order so you can observe the gradual development of the Impressionist Landscape series.

◀ NATURE AND ART COMBINE IN A SPECTACULAR SETTING.

I've always liked to read gardening and landscaping books. It's fun to imagine that someday my yard will bloom with as much color and vitality as those I see in the pictures. THE FLOWER BED was inspired by a photograph in a book entitled *The Flower Garden* by Richard Bisgrove. I didn't use the same types of flowers for my quilt, but I did use the angle of the flower bed and the proportion of the grassy area in the foreground to the darker foliage in the background.

THE FLOWER BED, 1991, 40″ X 41″, GAI PERRY

I found my inspiration for this quilt in a charming little book entitled *Monet's Passion* by Elizabeth Murray. Monet's passion, aside from painting, was cultivating his flowers. He planned his garden so he always had flowers to paint, no matter the season. My quilt is an interpretation of Monet's Grand Allee which is a nasturtium-lined pathway leading from his house to the gate at the front of the property.

MONET'S GARDEN, 1991, 53″ X 42″, GAI PERRY

$\mathcal{D}$uring the time I was painting, I worked in a style known as photographic realism. The only non-representational painting I ever did was an interpretation of Angel Falls, which, if I remember correctly, is in Africa. I used my painting as a reference for this quilt and chose a stark monochromatic blue and white color scheme.

FIRST WATERFALL, 1991, 44″ X 62″, GAI PERRY

$\mathcal{W}$henever I'm shown a photograph of THE TREE it's always presented to me upside down. It looks like a tree in full bloom, instead of a green-leafed tree with flowers nestling under the branches. Who's right? It probably does look better upside down.

THE TREE, 1991, 39″ X 41″, GAI PERRY

$\mathcal{T}$he colors in this quilt are pleasing to me, but in retrospect I wish I had pushed the design concept a little further. There is a sunny area of sky showing on the right side and I should have lightened a corresponding area in the hills and meadow.

FLOWERS GONE WILD, 1991, 46″ X 46″, GAI PERRY

*P*ANSIES was made with several color-ways of a realistic pansy print. I still have a good supply of these fabrics because it was one of the few times that I was smart enough to buy several yards at once. Usually when I go back to the store to purchase more fabric it's gone...never to be seen again (except in someone else's stash).

PANSIES, 1992, 23″ X 25″, GAI PERRY

$\mathcal{T}$his is a sample quilt for my two-day Meadow Landscape Workshop. I made a second meadow scene (COUNTRY MEADOWS shown on page 62) for this book so you could design the hills using a precise value-graded formula.

A DAY IN THE COUNTRY, 1992, 30″ X 36″, GAI PERRY

I designed this landscape quilt from a magazine photograph. I've never been to Montana but judging from the picture, it looks like a ruggedly handsome state full of natural beauty and pristine wilderness. I hear it's the newest "promised land" for Californians weary of smoggy cities and overcrowding. Sorry, Montana.

MONTANA SPRING, 1992, 63″ X 48″, GAI PERRY

$\mathcal{I}$ named this quilt BURPEE®: HYBRID MIX because it looks like it should be used for the cover of a seed catalog, or maybe even as an ad for fertilizer. Until I made this quilt I had worked with just a couple of square sizes but in order to make these flowers look as if they were planted in a garden, I figured out that I could use several size squares and rectangles to accommodate the various flower shapes. All the flowers come from one remarkable fabric.

BURPEE®: HYBRID MIX, 1992, 47″ X 36″, GAI PERRY

$\mathcal{W}$aterfalls, oceans, rivers, streams, brooks...
the sound of moving water raises my spirits. WATERFALL II was designed with an analogous color scheme (blue, blue-green, and yellow-green). A strong diagonal rhythm is established by the downward flow of the light value water. Also, an interesting counter-balance of the lighter value is created by the triangle of light arrangement. (Refer to page 17 for further definition.)

WATERFALL II, 1992, 38″ X 49″, GAI PERRY

*M*y inspiration was a schmaltzy romantic painting on the back of a postcard. The picture was pure Victoriana, but my quilt turned out to look like an overgrown medieval garden...probably because of the printed tapestry fabrics. When I finished this quilt, I felt like I was starting to make some progress with the landscape series. This design is more complex than anything I'd done before.

ANOTHER PATH TOWARD CAMELOT, 1992, 55″ X 52″, GAI PERRY

I couldn't have made SHORELINE if I hadn't found this wonderfully strange upholstery fabric. (Of course, beauty is in the eye of the beholder.) When I was buying it, the salesperson said, "I love this fabric. I just used it to make a bedspread for my son." The hills are composed of squares from the front of the fabric, and the foamy water and sea spray from the reverse side. The quilt is a representation of the West Coast shoreline. It could be anywhere from central California to Washington state. The wild flowers on the hills and the foggy sky are typical features of our western coast.

SHORELINE, 1993, 51″ X 42″, GAI PERRY

$\mathcal{M}$onet's waterlilies series was on my mind when I made this quilt. To make the lily pond section it took two and a half yards of one floral fabric because the flower I was using to create the lily pads was repeated only twice in every yard. All the fabrics in this quilt are used on the reverse side.

WATERLILIES, 1993, 28″ X 23″, GAI PERRY

I liked the first quilt so much that I made another. This time I had to use four yards of the floral fabric to complete the lily pond section. The gentle blue border gives this quilt a "softer" feeling.

WATERLILIES II, 1993, 33″ X 30″, GAI PERRY

I came across this very lovely floral print and it reminded me of one of Renoir's still-life paintings. The fabric was so painterly that it wouldn't blend with any other prints; I had to use it exclusively.

A RENOIR GARDEN, 1993, 32″ X 32″, GAI PERRY

*T*his is a larger version of THE FLOWER GARDEN on page 55. I wanted to expand the theme of a simple flower bed so I used some larger squares to provide a contrast of flower scale. When I was finished, I discovered that bigger is not necessarily better, and personally, I prefer the smaller garden quilt.

THE FLOWER GARDEN II, 1993, 60″ X 52″, GAI PERRY

*S*unflowers, iris, starry-night skies...elements from three of my favorite Van Gogh paintings are in this quilt. Many years ago I saw a collection of his work at the deYoung Museum in San Francisco. *WOW*! You can't begin to appreciate the explosive power and dazzling colors in his paintings until you see them in person. This quilt is my tribute to Vincent. The print scale of the fabrics seems larger than life with their own unique style…just like Van Gogh.

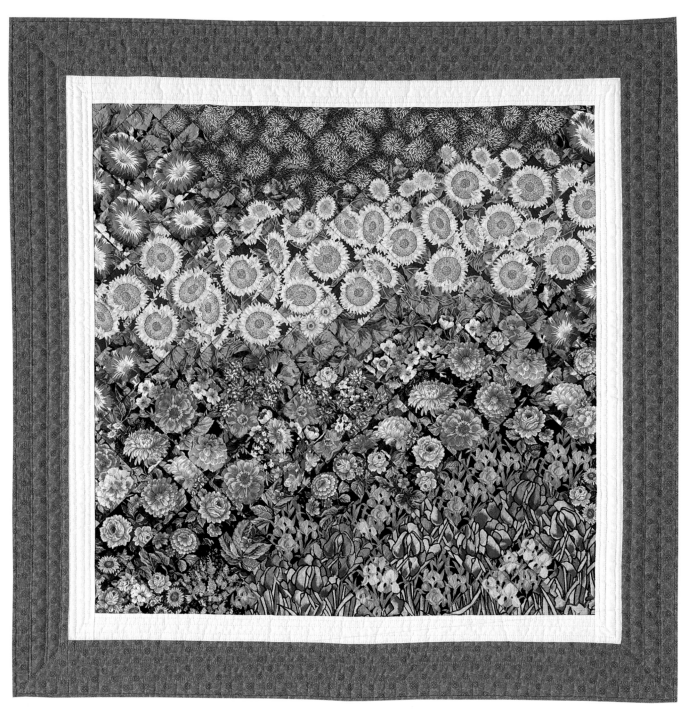

IF VINCENT HAD A GARDEN…, 1993, 48″ X 48″, GAI PERRY

$\mathcal{A}$nother waterfall! This is the biggest landscape
I've attempted so far. I had to climb up and down a step ladder to design it. Before I put it
together, it covered about seven vertical feet of my design wall.

WATERFALL III, 1993, 51″ X 66″, GAI PERRY

I had fun making this quilt. The fence is somewhat overpowering, but effective in a folk art sort of way. I think I was getting into my blue and yellow period. Do you see the morning glories on the right side? I think I used this fabric in almost every quilt I'd made in 1994.

AUGUST, 1994, 46″ X 42″, GAI PERRY

*H*ydrangeas are one of my favorite flowers. When I found a decorator-weight fabric covered with these blossoms, I had to use it. At first I was concerned about combining fabrics of different weights but I didn't have any problems with the quilting. Nor does the different thickness of the fabrics seem obvious.

TWILIGHT CREEK, 1994, 51″ X 51″, GAI PERRY

I wanted to design a lake but ran out of the
water fabric…I ended up with a pond. The day after I stitched the quilt top together,
more fabric arrived in the store. Isn't that just typical? Many of the flowers are the reverse
side of the fabric, giving this quilt a hazy, impressionistic feeling. Now that I have more of
the water fabric, I'd like to try this scene again using brighter flowers.

SUNRISE ON TURQUOISE POND, 1994, 43″ X 44″, GAI PERRY
MACHINE QUILTED BY MARGARET GAIR

*H*ere is good example of the gradual movement of pale to bright to darkly-shaded colors. If I had put a few of the flower squares from the upper left into the floral area on the lower right, they would have looked too obvious and out of place. But, by gradually moving toward the darker flowers, I was able to successfully incorporate tints, tones, and shades into the same quilt.

A SIMPLE COUNTRY HOUSE, 1994, 40″ X 42″, GAI PERRY
MACHINE QUILTED BY MARGARET GAIR

$\mathcal{H}$ere is another example of how to contrast bright and shaded flowers. I was using a grayed fabric with dramatically oversized blossoms, but it seemed the more squares I added, the duller my design became. When I introduced a few yellow-gold and lavender flowers of similar character, in somewhat brighter tones, the design improved remarkably. The quilt is named after William Morris—a famous artisan during the Arts & Crafts period. My quilt looks like a wallpaper print he might have designed.

A WILLIAM MORRIS GARDEN, 1994, 45″ X 48″, GAI PERRY

$\mathcal{C}$urrently, this is my favorite landscape. Aside from loving all the brilliant colors, it reminds me of summer. I'm a person who would be perfectly content to experience summer, with its long daylight hours, for eleven months of the year. That would leave me one month to enjoy all the orange, russet, and gold colors of fall.

GLORIOUS SUNFLOWERS, 1994, 54″ X 51″, GAI PERRY

Clockwise from top left: Vineyards, *Gai Perry*; Sunset, *John Barnett*; The Brook, *John Barnett*; Sunflowers, *Gai Perry*; Primroses, *Gai Perry*; Marsh, *John Barnett*

*I*NDEPENDENT STUDY

NOW THAT YOU HAVE A GROWING COLLECTION of flowers (no pun intended) and probably a few hundred leftover squares, you're almost obligated to make another landscape quilt. Now is the time to try an original design.

To start, you need an idea for a landscape that is so compelling you can hardly wait to begin cutting more squares. Perhaps the calendar hanging in your kitchen has a picture of an icy winter pond, or a desert at sunset, that starts your creative juices flowing. Look for inspiration everywhere: magazines, garden and travel books, home photographs. Once you've found a picture for your landscape, there are a few simple steps to complete before you begin working on your original design.

Step One: Draw a thumbnail sketch of the picture on graph paper. Simplify it by deleting elements that are impossible to achieve. Your sketch doesn't have to be a work of art. You just need a few lines to indicate the different areas.

THUMBNAIL SKETCH

Step Two: Determine the size you want your landscape to be by dividing the sketch into sixteen segments. To do this, fold the sketch lengthwise into fourths. Open it and then fold it into fourths across the width. Open it again and mark the creases with a pencil.

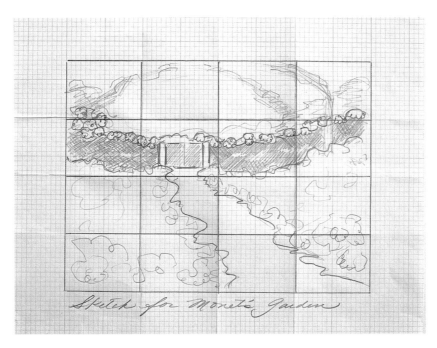

FOLDED THUMBNAIL SKETCH

You must decide how many squares you want to put on point in each segment. For example, assume that you want to put two squares on point vertically and three squares on point horizontally in each segment. Multiply the vertical number of squares in each segment by four to get a total of eight squares. Multiply the horizontal number of squares in each segment by four to get a total of twelve squares. Your landscape will have twelve squares on point across and eight squares on point down. Each square on point measures 2½″ after sewing, so your quilt, before the borders are added, will measure 30″ x 20″.

Step Three: Refer to the photograph of the square placement on page 123. Take a handful of leftover squares and place twelve of them point to point across the top of your design board. Place a total of eight squares, point to point, down the left and right sides of your design board. (Note: you must turn your design board sideways for this step.) Place twelve squares point to point across the bottom of the design board. This temporary arrangement of squares will indicate the perimeter of your landscape and will tell you whether or not your proposed design will fit. Your flannel design board will accommodate eleven squares horizontally and thirteen squares vertically. If your design is too big, you will either have to adjust it or make a larger design surface. I've created a design wall in my sewing room by stapling (don't gasp—the holes are tiny) two 45″ widths of 5 oz. fleece on my wall, starting at the ceiling and working toward the floor, just like wallpapering. This gives me a design area that measures seven and a half feet across by eight feet down.

SQUARE PLACEMENT

Step Four: Gather fabrics for each element and arrange them in a large fan shape so you can decide whether or not the colors have a harmonious relationship. Fabric selection will be on-going throughout the design phase but these should be enough to get you started.

Are you ready? Take a deep breath and begin your original landscape. Don't be intimidated by your empty design board and don't try finishing your landscape in a day. You're aiming for product, not assembly-line processing. Take pleasure in the gradual blending of colors and textures. Feel the beauty and individual character of your landscape as it slowly evolves and takes shape. Cut out a few squares and start designing in an area that feels comfortable. I like to start at the center of the horizon and work outward in all directions. The segmented sketch on page 122 is a guide to the general location of each element in your landscape.

Your design experience will be more enjoyable if you don't lock yourself into too many preconceived ideas, or a concept that is too difficult to achieve. I've yet to make a wall hanging that turned out looking like the original plan. Each landscape seems to develop its own life. I just go with the flow.

Emphasize fabrics that are working and delete fabrics (even if they're favorites) that don't blend. When you get frustrated, or stuck in a particular area, take a break. Go for a walk, do a load of laundry…or, my personal preference is to have a nice cup of tea and a chocolate chip cookie.

As your landscape grows, know that you are creating an original work of art. It's yours alone, and no one else can complete it in exactly the same way. Enjoy!

TEMPLATES

ALL THE TEMPLATE PATTERNS are based on multiples of the 1¾″ finished square. With this assortment, you will have the flexibility to cut just about any size flower (or group of flowers). The rectangular shapes are perfect for flowers such as tulips and iris. Replace some of the squares in the design with rectangles to add variety to the quilt. For example, one small rectangle equals two 2¼″ squares and one large rectangle equals three 2¼″ squares.

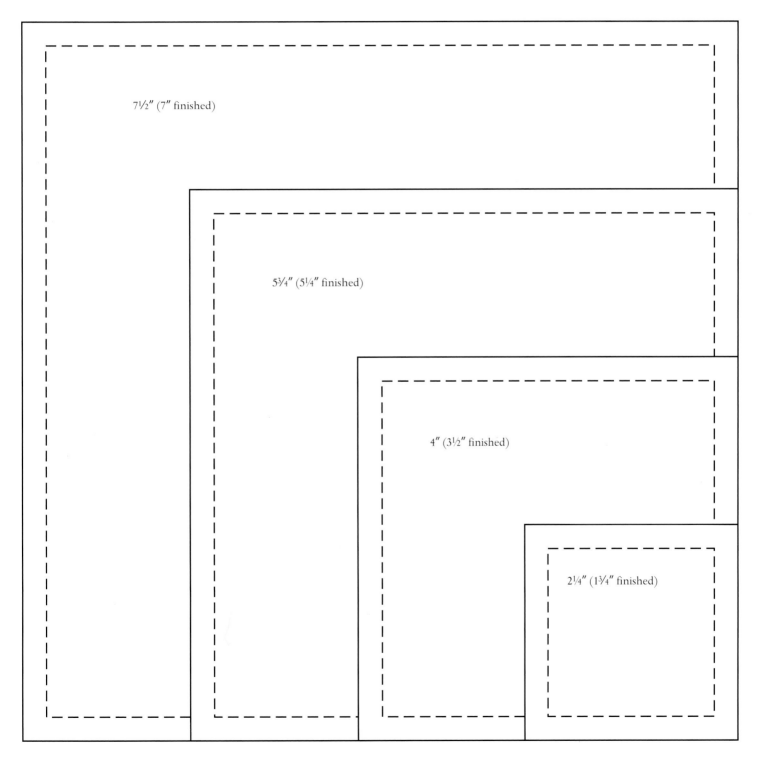

7½″ (7″ finished)

5¾″ (5¼″ finished)

4″ (3½″ finished)

2¼″ (1¾″ finished)

¼″ seam allowances are already added to all the template patterns.

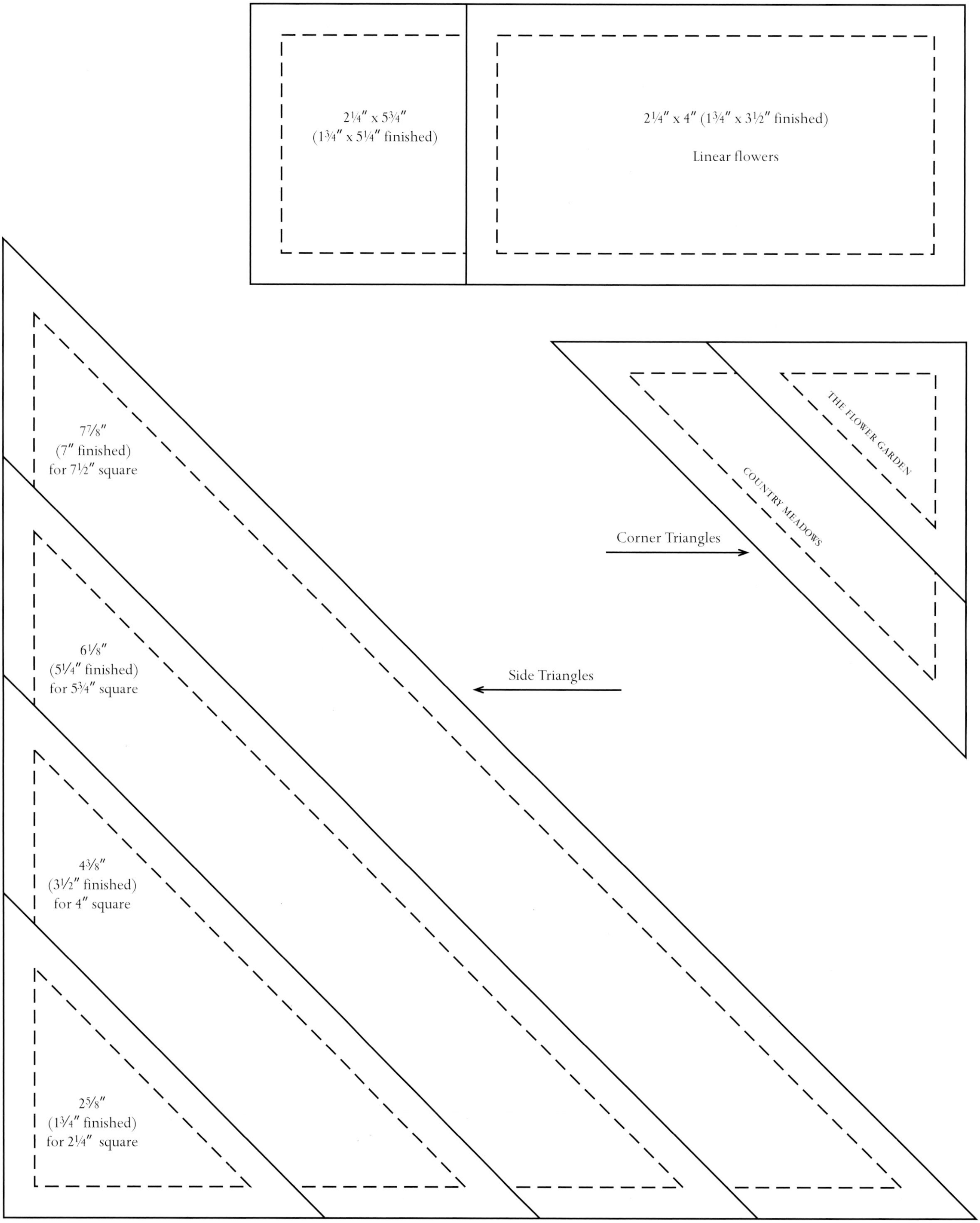

2¼″ x 5¾″
(1¾″ x 5¼″ finished)

2¼″ x 4″ (1¾″ x 3½″ finished)

Linear flowers

7⅞″
(7″ finished)
for 7½″ square

6⅛″
(5¼″ finished)
for 5¾″ square

4⅜″
(3½″ finished)
for 4″ square

2⅝″
(1¾″ finished)
for 2¼″ square

Corner Triangles

Side Triangles

COUNTRY MEADOWS

THE FLOWER GARDEN

BIBLIOGRAPHY

Birren, Faber. *Creative Color*
West Chester, PA: Schiffer Publishing Ltd., 1987

De Grandis. *Theory and Use of Color*
New York: Harry N. Abrams, Inc., 1986

Itten, Johannes. *The Elements of Color*
New York: Van Nostrand Reinhold Company, 1970

Joyes, Claire. *Claude Monet, Life at Giverny*
New York: The Vendome Press, 1985

Basic Quilting Techniques

McClun, Diana and Nownes, Laura. *Quilt!, Quilts!!, Quilts!!! The Complete Guide to Quiltmaking*
San Francisco: The Quilt Digest Press, 1988

McClun, Diana and Nownes, Laura. *Quilts, Quilts, and More Quilts!*
Lafayette, CA: C&T Publishing, 1993

Art and Gardening Books with Inspirational Photographs

Bisgrove, Richard. *The Flower Garden*
New York: Penguin Books, 1989

Dixon, Trisha. *The Country Garden*
New York: Harper Collins Publisher, 1992

Fell, Derek. *The Impressionist Garden*
New York: Carol Southern Books, 1994

Greenoak, Francesca. *Glorious Gardens*
New York: Congdon & Weed, Inc., 1989

House, John. *Monet, Nature into Art*
New Haven: Yale University Press, 1986

McGuire, Diane Kostal. *Gardens of America—Three Centuries of Design*
Charlottesville, NC: Thomasson-Grant, Inc., 1989

Murray, Elizabeth. *Monet's Passion*
San Francisco: Pomegranate Artbooks, 1989

Trenton, Patricia and Gerdts, William H. *California Light 1900–1930*
San Francisco: Bedford Art Publishers, 1990

ABOUT THE AUTHOR

GAI PERRY DISCOVERED THE ART OF QUILTMAKING in 1981. Just for the fun of it, she took a beginner's course one day and fell in love with this enchanting craft. Six months later she closed her antique shop, and she's been happily quilting ever since.

In 1985, Gai started teaching quilting at local shops and quilt seminars throughout California and Oregon. Her early seminars focused on the effective use of color and fabric in traditional quilts. But by 1990, she had developed an original style of contemporary quilt design which she calls "The Art of the Impressionist Landscape." These Impressionist Landscape quilts are the happy marriage of Gai's love of painting and quilt design. She now works exclusively on this series. This effective how-to book, *Impressionist Quilts,* is the result of four years of Gai's design exploration and teaching the Impressionist Landscape technique. Gai attributes her artistic gift to the fact that her family gene pool overflows with artists and craftsmen.

For a complete list of Other Fine Books from C&T Publishing, write for a free catalog:
P.O. Box 1456, Lafayette, CA 94549. Or call toll free 1.800.284.1114.